DATE			

Writing Baseball

THE SOUTHERN ILLINOIS UNIVERSITY PRESS SERIES

Other Books in the Writing Baseball Series

Full Count

FULL COUNT
Inside Cuban Baseball

MILTON H. JAMAIL

With a Foreword by Larry Dierker

Southern Illinois University Press
Carbondale and Edwardsville

Library of Congress Cataloging-in-Publication Data
Jamail, Milton H.
Full count : inside Cuban baseball / Milton H. Jamail with a foreword by Larry Dierker.
p. cm. — (Writing baseball)
Includes bibliographical references and index.
1. Baseball—Cuba. 2. Baseball—Social aspects—Cuba.
I. Title. II. Series.
GV863.25.A1J26 2000
796.357'097291—dc21   99-40409
ISBN 0-8093-2310-9 (cloth)   CIP

The paper used in this publication meets the minimum requirements of American National
Standard for Information Sciences—Permanence of Paper for Printed Library Materials,
ANSI Z39.48-1992. ♾

Writing Baseball Series Editor: Richard Peterson

To the members of the Peña Deportiva Parque Central,

especially Marcelo Sánchez and Asdrubal Baró,

and to Ernesto "Chico" Morilla,

all of whom shared with me their knowledge of

and passion for baseball

CONTENTS

Illustrations following page 46

FOREWORD
Larry Dierker

I first met Milton Jamail in the spring of 1965, my rookie year. He was a student at the University of Houston and a baseball fan. I was an eighteen-year-old pitcher with the Astros. We did not stay in contact, but in the summer of 1987 Milton showed up in the press box at the Astrodome. My longtime friend, Bill Worrell, who was also at the University of Houston in 1965 and who is now an Astros broadcaster, introduced me to Milton for the second time. Milton admitted that he had lost track of baseball for twenty years or so while he was pursuing his doctorate. When he started traveling in the Caribbean, the baseball bug got him again. Now as a professor at the University of Texas, he can mix business with pleasure. I think you will enjoy the firstborn of that marriage, *Full Count*.

When I learned Milton was working on a history of baseball in the Caribbean region, I was full of questions. I have been harboring a notion to write a novel about Winterball since I returned from pitching in the Dominican Republic in the 1967–68 season. I thought Milton's book would be my guide, but after ten years, I was beginning to have doubts.

"When is the opus due?" I would ask him.

"Still working on it."

"In this lifetime?"

"Maybe."

Suddenly, from the midst of the unfinished book, Cuba raised its hirsute head and demanded attention.

Milton has been spreading seeds and harvesting information throughout the Caribbean for the past ten years. *Full Count* is just a hint of what is to come. It is a timely work, in view of the current sociopolitical situation in Cuba and the recent exhibition between the Baltimore Orioles and a Cuban all-star team. And while it is timely, it is also, like baseball, timeless. It reveals Milton's passion for baseball and for its Spanish-speaking players. It also reflects the thorough and thoughtful nature of his academic training. It is the blending that makes the book so appealing. It is about art and politics. It's about the graceful lines of baseball and the hard reality of poverty. It provides a framework for understanding the importance of baseball in Cuba, from the way it is organized from the youth leagues up to the Cuban national team, and the way it is utilized by Fidel Castro as a symbol of excellence and a voice for the rallying cry of nationalism. *Full Count* reads more like a story than a text. And it has a style that is as comfortable as a well-worn glove.

When Milton handed me the manuscript, I was afraid I was getting a dry-cleaned thesis paper. I should have known better. When Milton talks *béisbol* he really gets excited and his dark eyes start to sparkle. He tells you about Latin players you've never heard of, sixteen- and seventeen-year-old youngsters who have not yet left their native soil in search of the American baseball dream. He offers inside information about current big leaguers. This guy, he might say, is very bright. He will come on fast. This player is immature. He'll never get much better than he is right now. Or this player grew up with eleven brothers and sisters and had to fight for everything he got. It is the human side of the game that stirs Milton's juices. And it is precisely that aspect of the Latin baseball experience that comes through in this book.

Milton comes into Houston from Austin on the weekends until school lets out in mid-May. After that, he sees more games both here in the Astrodome and further south in the Caribbean. When he is on the field during batting practice in the Dome, he spends most of his time interviewing Spanish-speaking players from both the Astros and the visiting club. Watching his facial expressions and the reactions of the players, it is clear that he is getting through, forming alliances, and cultivating sources. The sparkle in his eye turns into a wildfire when he visits with players he has known since they were teenagers like Richard Hidalgo. The Spanish-speaking ballplayers seem to speak louder and gesticulate more than their North American counterparts. Milton too becomes more animated when he is speaking Spanish.

Baseball is the central symbol of Cuban pride. And until lately, Castro has been able to stir the island nation into a popular frenzy with images of the almost flawless record of the Cuban national team. In the early 1990s, things started to change. In 1991, René Arocha defected and signed with the St. Louis Cardinals. In 1997, Cuba finally lost a game in official international competition. While the national team has improved since then, the government is still concerned about defection when the team travels abroad. Milton is not a social crusader, but his frustration over the fate of the Cuban ballplayer jumps from these pages. This book helps us understand why the decision to leave is so difficult for Cuban players.

What will come of the series between the Cuban all-stars and the Baltimore Orioles? Who will win the battle in our own Congress over lifting the trade embargo? What will the rapidly increasing influx of tourist dollars do to the Cuban economy? How long will Castro live and what will happen when he dies? How long can this island, which is so close to the United States, remain so far away? No one, not even my friend Milton Jamail, knows the answers to these questions. But his study of baseball in Cuba gives the reader insight into the country's national sport and a glimpse of life on the island. If you are a baseball fan, a potential tourist, or just a person who likes a good cigar, you will take pleasure in this account.

PREFACE

When I began researching and writing about the relationship between Latin American and U.S. professional baseball in the late 1980s, I had no intention of writing a book about Cuban baseball. At that time there were few Cuban players in the major leagues, and those few there were had grown up in the United States.

I had maintained a long interest in Cuba and had often taught college courses on U.S.-Cuban political relations. In 1991, my credentials as a journalist, coupled with my ability to speak Spanish, allowed me to visit with *equipo Cuba*—the Cuban national team—when they played a series against the U.S. team in Millington, Tennessee. I was awed by the level of talent. It seemed clear that someday Cuba would again send its best players to the U.S. professional leagues.

I began to accumulate clippings on Cuban baseball, collect rosters of Cuban teams as they played in international competition, and write short articles on Cuban baseball for *USA Today Baseball Weekly*. In 1992, I went to Cuba with the U.S. Olympic baseball team for a four-game series against *equipo Cuba*. I was getting closer to the heart of Cuban baseball, but I still envisioned Cuba as being only a chapter in a larger book on Latin American baseball.

In early 1997, *Baseball Weekly* asked me to go to Cuba for a week with writer Tim Wendel to assess the current state of Cuban baseball. It was an incredible trip. Not only did I renew old acquaintances in Cuban baseball, but I began to more clearly understand the relationship between baseball and the economic crisis in Cuba, and the state of U.S.-Cuba relations. As I typed my notes and wrote the articles from that trip, I realized that the story of Cuban baseball was becoming more important and that I was in a unique position to write about it. I began to receive numerous calls from members of both the print and the electronic media—from the *New York Times* to the British Broadcasting Corporation—asking basic questions about baseball in Cuba.

I traveled to Cuba in December 1997, March 1998, and January and March 1999, each visit lasting from a week to ten days, and talked day and night to Cubans at every level about the current state of baseball. When I returned from Cuba in March 1998, I had two phone messages. One was from a producer at CBS to let me know that the *60 Minutes* segment I had taped with Morley Safer in January would air in the next two weeks. The second was from the CIA. An employee there had heard from a colleague, a University of Texas alum, that I was writing a book. She asked if I'd fly to Washington to give a briefing to twenty or so of their analysts. A briefing? I explained that I was only writing about baseball. She responded that they were interested in all aspects of Cuba. I politely declined, adding that I planned to return to Cuba to complete my research, and I didn't think the Cubans would understand my briefing the CIA between trips. But I suggested that they buy my book when it was published and at that point, if they had questions, I'd be happy to answer them.

I have been able to take a close look at Cuban baseball from the inside: a view afforded few foreign journalists or researchers. During the 1990s, I made six trips to Cuba and met with baseball officials, coaches, managers, players, and fans, as well as with many Cuban journalists assigned to cover their national sport. In a country where substantial critical discourse is prohibited, where the press and media are controlled by the government, and where most people have to struggle day to day to "resolve" their difficult financial situations, baseball provides excitement, provokes laughter, incites spirited debate, and gives most Cubans something to be proud of: *equipo Cuba*, the national team that represents their country in international tournaments. While most Cubans are eager to discuss their national sport, Cuban sports officials and players are not. It is easy to understand their reluctance because they have little to gain and much to lose by talking to a foreigner, especially when he happens to be a journalist.

In this book, I attempt to explain why Cubans are so good at playing baseball; explore the deep roots and love of the game on the island;

describe the state of Cuban baseball today, including a detailed description of the formation of the Cuban baseball system after the 1959 revolution; discuss the decline in quality of the Cuban national baseball team over the last few years, in part due to the defection of some of the country's top players; examine the tremendous interest of U.S. major league teams in Cuba; and analyze the changes necessary, both in Cuba and in the United States, to facilitate the return of Cuban players to U.S. baseball.

There are simply too many people who have contributed to this book to list individually. But I do want to express my appreciation to everyone in Cuba who helped me, from the men in the Parque Central in Havana to the government officials who shared their insights on their national sport. Special thanks go to Peter Katel, Alan Klein, Tom Miller, Bartholomew Sparrow, and Tim Wendel, all of whom read and offered comments on various drafts of the manuscript. Thanks also go to Joseph Arbena, Peter Bjarkman, Roberto González Echevarría, Aline Helg, Rick Lawes, and Sonia Labrador Rodríguez, all of whom provided suggestions and support at various stages of the project. Support for my trip to Cuba in 1992 was provided by the Institute of Latin American Studies at the University of Texas at Austin from funds granted to the institute by the Andrew W. Mellon Foundation. The entire project would not have been possible without the constant support and inspiration of my wife, Margo Gutiérrez. She read and commented on every draft of the manuscript and encouraged me to share my passion for Cuban baseball with others.

Full Count

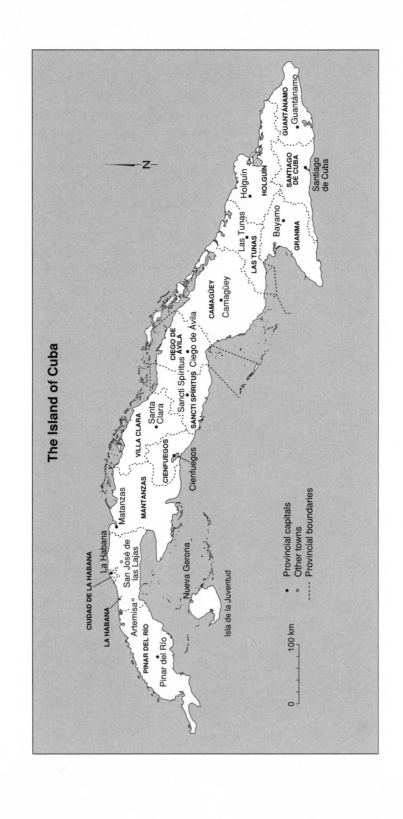

The Island of Cuba

1 ☆ Cuban Baseball and the United States

"You grow up with baseball all around you," Javier Méndez, an outfielder for the hometown Industriales, told me as he was preparing for a game in Havana's Estadio Latinoamericano. "It is part of being Cuban. Baseball is one of the roots of Cuban reality." And as Sigfredo Barros, the baseball beat writer since the mid-1980s for *Granma*, Cuba's official government newspaper, explained, "In Cuba, baseball is more than a sport. It is part of the culture; it is part of our national pride."

It is difficult to find a family in Cuba that does not include a member who loves baseball. Wherever one goes in Cuba, there are young boys playing baseball, and people talk about the game constantly in every corner of the island. Baseball even influences the way the people talk. "When something goes wrong, you might say to a friend, 'They caught you off base,' or to a person who is nervous, 'You've lost control, you need to throw a strike.' And when someone is facing a difficult situation, he is *en 3 y 2* [facing a full count]," explained Miguel Valdés who, until 1997, was technical director of *equipo Cuba*—the Cuban national team.

The Cubans have a great term for a rhubarb. They call it a *cámara húngara*, named after the heated discussions in the Hungarian Parliament during the 1930s. Also, when I asked for the Cuban equivalent of *donnybrook*, I was told it is the common slang word for a brawl, *bronca*. It is, coincidentally, the same word the Cubans use to describe

1

the bizarre relations they've had with the U.S. government over the past forty years.

One hundred thirty-five Cubans have played in the U.S. major leagues, most between 1947, when the game was integrated, and 1961, when Fidel Castro abolished professional baseball. When the United States severed diplomatic relations with Cuba in 1961, the major leagues' main source of foreign players was cut off. With all of its talent now at home, Cuba became a powerhouse in amateur baseball, winning almost every international competition, including Olympic gold medals in Barcelona in 1992 and in Atlanta in 1996.

In 1991, a few Cuban players began to defect and play professional baseball in the United States, but it was not until the performance of Florida Marlins pitcher Liván Hernández in the 1997 post-season and the success of Orlando Hernández with the Yankees in 1998 that the U.S. media began to take notice of Cuban players' potential to reinvigorate baseball in the United States. When Liván Hernández struck out fifteen Atlanta Braves batters in the 1997 National League Championship Series, baseball fans in the United States were surprised, and when the rookie Cuban defector went on to win the MVP in the World Series, fans wondered whether there were more players like him back in Cuba. When his half-brother, Orlando "El Duque" Hernández, was smuggled off the island in a small boat at the end of 1997, Cuban baseball became front-page news. In 1998, "El Duque" signed a four-year, $6.6-million contract with the New York Yankees in March, made his major league debut in June, and earned a victory in the World Series in October.

Although Cuba has been off-limits to Major League Baseball for almost forty years, all thirty clubs look forward to the possibility of once again having access to Cuban players. For the baseball industry, Cuba represents the most important frontier in the increasingly important global search for players. Shortly after the turn of the century, Cuba will likely become the number one source of foreign-born players for the U.S. big leagues.

Baseball was neither imposed on the Cuban people before 1959 nor delivered by the triumph of the Cuban Revolution. For more than 125 years, baseball in the United States and baseball in Cuba have been intertwined. The first Latino in U.S. professional baseball was Cuban Estéban Bellán, who played with the Troy Haymakers in 1872, and

U.S. major league teams played exhibition games in Cuba as early as 1890. African Americans played in Cuba at the turn of the century, and Cuban blacks, excluded from Major League Baseball, played in the U.S. Negro Leagues. After Jackie Robinson broke the color barrier in 1947, dark-skinned Cubans such as Orestes "Minnie" Miñoso were actively recruited.

While it seems clear that Cubans will return in large numbers, don't start putting Cuban players on your rotisserie club roster just yet. There are still two major hurdles. First, the Cuban government clings to an ideology of no professionalism in sports. Because of this prohibition, once a player leaves Cuba, he cannot go back. And second, the U.S. embargo and the Trading with the Enemies Act prohibit U.S. organizations from any dealings with Cuba and keep Cuban ballplayers from taking their salaries home.

So Close . . .

"I could see the lights of Havana directly ahead [and] the lights of the Florida Keys curved like a string of fireflies off to the northeast," recalls former U.S. diplomat Wayne Smith about a flight from Miami. But he notes, "the nearness had been an illusion. Only minutes apart and on a clear night visible to the same eye, the United States and Cuba were nonetheless separated by an immense gulf."[1]

Although Cuba and the United States are only ninety miles apart, the island could just as well be on the other side of the world. Until recently, people in the United States had little or no information about contemporary Cuba. In general, Cubans know a bit more about the United States than their American counterparts know about Cuba. But for the most part, in the absence of formal diplomatic relations between the two countries and in the face of the hostility of the U.S. government toward the regime of Fidel Castro, people in either country during the past forty years have relied on past images of each other or on images constructed by their respective governments.

Even though Cuba has dominated international amateur baseball since the mid-1960s and has done so in the shadow of the United States, Cuba's accomplishments remain obscured. Many reporters visiting Cuba look for exotic traits of the game there, and while Cuba is exotic and foreign, Cuban baseball is not. The rules are the same: nine men on a side, nine innings in a game, and sixty feet six inches from the pitcher's mound to home plate. Cuba used aluminum bats (for economic reasons) and the designated hitter (because the International Baseball Association uses it). While some terms, such as "home club," "double play," "hit" (*jit*), "strike," "hit-and-run," and "squeeze play" (*equiplay*), carry over from English, the positions are most often translated into Spanish. The infield, from first to third, consists of *primera* or *inicialista, segunda* or *camarero* (literally meaning "waiter"), and *tercera* or *antisalista*. The shortstop is "short" (spelled *siol* in Cuba) or *torpedero*. Outfielders are called *jardineros* (gardeners) and may be referred to in either language: for example, "center fielder" or *jardinero central*. The catcher is the *receptor*, and the pitcher is the *lanzador* or *serpentinero*, named after the streamers thrown at parties.

One difference a U.S. fan would notice while watching baseball in Cuba is that the first time a batter comes to the plate in a game, he will shake hands with the catcher and umpire. Another significant difference is that fans are loyal to teams based on seeing the same players year after year; there is no free agency in Cuba.

Then there are the names. A glance at the rosters of Cuba's development league—taxi squads to the teams in Cuba's main baseball circuit that are composed of players under age twenty-three—reveals names such as Yobal, Yuleski, Yosandry, Yohankis, Yoelsis, Yohandris, Yohanet, Yunier, and Yanier. And there are Yoelvis, Orelvis and, of course, Elvis. I asked Raúl Arce who, since the late 1960s, has been a reporter for *Juventud Rebelde*, a weekly newspaper, why there are so many unusual names among Cuban players. Like *Granma*'s Barros, Arce is a baseball beat writer, except that his beat includes all age groups. You might find Arce at the all-star game for the Cuban big leagues or at a tournament for fifteen- to sixteen-year-olds. When he travels abroad, it is usually with the younger teams. "It's hard to find any young people named José, Raúl, or Juan in Cuba today," remarked Arce, not really explaining why this phenomenon occurs, "and when you think about the unusual names, you have the famous case of the woman living in Guantánamo in the 1950s who named her son 'Usnavy' after seeing a U.S. plane fly overhead. Another good one is 'Norge,' named after the American freezers. And then there was a time when there were a lot of Russian names like Vladimir, but that period is over."

Many fans in the United States want to know when Cuban players will return to play in professional baseball. Few are pleased with a necessarily imprecise answer, and even fewer are satisfied with an explanation that involves the complex political history of the two countries. However, it is essential to understand some basic facts about the recent political history of Cuba and U.S.-Cuban diplomatic relations of the past forty years to adequately comprehend why U.S.-Cuban baseball relations are so convoluted. Baseball also provides a window to view both the current economic crisis and the difficult transition to a new economy and, eventually, a new political order and a new relationship with the United States.

The Dollarization of Cuba

Traveling to Cuba is not easy, is rarely predictable, and is always exciting. Because of the Trading with the Enemies Act, U.S. citizens—with the exception of Cuban Americans on family visits, full-time journalists, and academics who request a special license from the U.S. Department of the Treasury—are not allowed to travel to the island. Those persons traveling to Cuba who don't fall into the aforementioned categories are subject to steep fines and prison terms. Most trips to Cuba begin in Havana, and going to the Cuban capital is like going back in time. Even in its current state of disrepair, Havana is one of the most beautiful and romantic cities in the world. Unlike most other Caribbean destinations, there are no tour ships arriving daily.

Since the early 1990s, Cuba is a society in disintegration, and few, if any, of its residents have the slightest idea of where it is going. But the Cuban people, even in the midst of an economic crisis, are outgoing and cordial. Most are genuinely interested in discussing the United States and are extremely courteous to the few Americans they encounter.

On my first visit in 1979 as a tourist (permitted by a relaxation of travel restrictions during the Carter administration), I saw a country that was justifiably proud of its accomplishments—particularly in education and health care—and whose citizens, compared to other countries in Latin America, were relatively well-off. Aid from the Soviet Union, while not compensating for the losses caused by the U.S. embargo, did cushion the shock and enabled Cubans to maintain a vision of better days ahead.

When I returned in July 1992 with the U.S. Olympic baseball team, I was appalled. I saw a Cuba that had come to a standstill. In the wake of the Soviet Union's collapse, Cuba was struggling to survive. Cuba was in the *período especial* (special period), which was the excuse used for broken machinery and lack of goods and services. On that trip I went to Holguín, a city of 250,000 residents situated five hundred miles to the east of Havana, for a U.S.-Cuba baseball series. I cannot recall seeing a passenger car on the street during my three-day stay there. In Havana, there was also very little traffic on the streets and nothing to buy in the stores. There were frequent electrical black-outs, and there was aggressive prostitution—unlike anything I had seen in thirty years of travel in Latin America. Why, I asked, did the government object to selling the contracts of baseball players, while it seemed to have no problem letting young Cubans sell their bodies?

As the Cuban economy entered a free fall, the government latched on to whatever it could for national pride and prestige. Baseball was its main asset. Whatever else, at least Cuba had the best amateur baseball team in the world.

When I returned in 1997, I expected to find a slightly different Cuba than the one I left four-and-a-half years earlier, but I was not prepared for the drastic changes I encountered. In 1993, the Cuban government began to allow the circulation of U.S. dollars. Now there was wonderful Cuban food available in restaurants and in *paladares* (small family eateries). Almost anything was available for U.S. dollars, but the only Cubans with access to dollars were people who worked in the tourist industry, sold handicrafts in street markets, or received dollars from family and friends overseas.

In 1998 and 1999, I saw a society even more divided between those with access to dollars and those who had to struggle to obtain the basic elements necessary for survival. Even medications prescribed by physicians in Cuba's highly touted health-care system had to be purchased in dollars. This "dollarization" was necessary to stop the economic free fall of the Cuban economy, but it also introduced a dynamic that is difficult for the Cuban government to control. By 1997, U.S. dollars brought to the island either by tourists or through remittances—money sent to Cuba by family members living off the island—had far surpassed sugar as the number one source of foreign exchange for Cuba. Much of the dollar economy is controlled by hustlers who offer tourists everything from black-market cigars to prostitutes, while those citizens who remain loyal to the decaying socialist system and continue to support the Revolution are left out in the cold. While in the recent past the Cuban economy might have been miserable, the difficulties were, for the most part, shared collectively. Today, there are sharp cleavages in Cuban society, and those with access to dollars suffer less than those without access. More important, there is a growing sense in Cuba that the collective advances of the Cuban people have broken down into an individual struggle for survival. The sign on the left field wall in the Estadio Latinoamericano—Havana's main ballpark—proclaiming *Somos de la misma casa* (We are all from the same house) clearly was wishful thinking.

How does this situation relate to Cuban baseball? The bottom line is that since Cuba legalized dollars in 1993, the position of baseball players in Cuban society has gone from privileged to underprivileged. Cuban players receive only a small salary, less than the equivalent of $30 a month, but it takes at least $120 a month to sustain a basic level of comfort in Havana. Cuban musicians and artists are allowed to come and go—and to bring dollars back into the country. University professors and medical doctors can become waiters in tourist hotels, hawk wares to tourists on the street, or bake cookies to sell to neighbors— and earn dollars. Baseball players are effectively excluded from this sector of the economy, and if they receive money from the United States, they become suspect for fear they are planning to defect. They must remain poor and above suspicion.

When *equipo Cuba* lost the title game at the Intercontinental Cup in Barcelona in 1997, breaking a ten-year undefeated streak in official international competitions, some observers in the United States attributed the decline in Cuban baseball to the defections that began when pitcher René Arocha left in 1991. But the two main problems facing Cuban baseball are, ironically, Cuba's abundance of players with little possibility of advancement and the unwillingness of the Cuban government to provide the necessary economic stimulus for players to remain in the country. When the government allowed some players to "retire," play in amateur leagues overseas, and bring home a portion of their earnings, it recognized the nature of the problem. But Cuba's very discerning and demanding fans missed some of their star players and quickly noticed the decline in play in the Serie Nacional, and they stayed away in droves.

The problems the government encounters in baseball are linked to every other aspect of the crisis facing Cuban society and cannot be solved through a quick fix. The situation poses a challenge for the Cuban government that is not easily surmounted. If Cuba is to remain a world baseball power, Cuban teams must travel outside of the country. And when they do, the government runs the risk of players not returning. The temptation is, of course, to select players not likely to defect, but the result is a national team not selected entirely on athletic ability. As one Cuban fan told the *New York Times*, "It's not enough to be a good guy and a good comrade. You've got to perform too."

One logical but currently impossible solution would be to allow the players to go to the United States. The best baseball in the world is played in the heart of the island's principal enemy. And even if the Cuban government encouraged its players to go to the United States, because of the blockade they could do so only as defectors. Baseball also has become *parte de la bronca*.

The Revolution of 1959

Although many in the United States think of Cuba as a small island ruled by Fidel Castro that produces exquisite cigars and magnificent baseball players—neither of which has free access to the U.S. market—the reality is more complex. In fact, Cuba is not small. Although its widest section is only about 75 miles, the island stretches in length some 750 miles—about the same distance as between New York City and Chicago. Its almost 12 million people are a blend of European- and African-origin populations. They live both in large cities such as Havana, with a population of 2.5 million, and spread out across the beautiful countryside, which is dotted by palm trees. While tobacco is the crop many Americans would like to freely savor, sugar dominates the island's history.

Cuba became one of Spain's first colonies in the New World in the early 1500s. In 1902, it was also the last country to receive its independence from Spain. Cuba was dominated by the United States, first with the occupying forces during the Spanish-American War, then by the Platt Amendment, which allowed the United States to intervene directly in the internal affairs of the island's government. Significantly, in 1959, Cuba became the first country in Latin America to define the interests of its own people ahead of the interests of foreign investors.

Although the revolutionary forces led by Fidel Castro did not take control of the Cuban government until January 2, 1959, the struggle to overthrow the dictatorship of Fulgencio Batista began almost six years earlier. On July 26, 1953, Fidel and a group of 165 revolutionaries attacked the Moncada military barracks in the eastern city of Santiago de Cuba. Historians have described the attack as daring and spectacular. Although it was a failure, it propelled Fidel Castro into the leadership of the armed opposition.[2] "The nation was horrified by the governmental repression and moved by the daring, if reckless, action of the young Cubans," notes historian Marifeli Pérez-Stable. "Fidel Castro especially captured the popular imagination."[3]

After the overthrow of Batista on January 1, 1959, Fidel's revolutionary agenda soon brought Cuba into a collision course with the United States. By January 1961, the United States broke diplomatic relations with Cuba, and they have not been reestablished. Soon after, in April 1961, the United States sponsored an attempt to overthrow the Castro government. The Bay of Pigs debacle was based on the faulty premise that Cubans on the island would rally around an invading force. Although the invasion failed, the Cuban government's understanding that the United States would continue to undermine the gains made by the new government brought about a closer relationship between Cuba and the Soviet Union. This relationship led to the Cuban Missile Crisis of October 1962, which brought the world to the edge of nuclear war.

The focus of the antagonistic relationship between the United States and Cuba is Fidel Castro. Now in his fortieth year in power, Fidel at age seventy-three has outlasted eight U.S. presidents—Eisenhower, Kennedy, Johnson, Nixon, Ford, Carter, Reagan, and Bush—and may still be in charge when Clinton leaves office. In addition to the Bay of Pigs attempt, the U.S. government has been involved in efforts to destroy sectors of Cuban agricultural and livestock production and has hatched several plots to embarrass and even assassinate Fidel. "Castro's continuing interest in baseball was noted by the CIA and became the basis for some of the agency's assassination plans," wrote former U.S. Senator Eugene McCarthy. "Our operatives tried first to get him to play catch with a baseball loaded with explosives."[4] Another plot had the CIA spraying LSD in a Havana television studio to make it appear that Fidel had gone mad while addressing the Cuban people. Yet another effort involved the CIA's contamination of a box of Fidel's favorite cigars in 1960 "with a botulinum toxin so potent that a person would die after putting one in his mouth."[5] The cigars were never delivered.

In addition, the United States has maintained an embargo on Cuba for almost forty years, even though at the end of the century, the United States is the one now isolated. While most nations of the world—including our two closest neighbors, Canada and Mexico—openly trade with Cuba, in 1997 the United States began to tighten the embargo with the passing of the Helms-Burton Law.

Why Does Major League Baseball Need to Import Players?

The baseball industry, like most other multinational enterprises, does not confine itself within the borders of one country. While some U.S. major league teams go into Latin America, Asia, Australia, and Europe as a cost-cutting measure, the baseball industry also must recruit talent overseas because it suffers from a shortage of quality players at home. Some analysts believe that sports talent in the United States is spread too thin, with U.S. youngsters playing basketball, football, volleyball and increasingly, soccer, in addition to baseball. Others see kids in the United States as too pampered, unwilling to put in the long hours and hard work necessary for success in baseball and choosing instead to spend their afternoons playing video games or watching television. Whatever the reasons, the talent pool for baseball in the United States clearly is shrinking, thus making it necessary to look elsewhere for players. To be competitive today, almost all major league organizations consider active participation in the Latin market—basically, the Dominican Republic, Venezuela, Mexico, and Panama—essential, and many scouts believe Cuba will be the cornerstone of that market.

Strip away the forty-year-old political impasse between the United States and Cuba and two facts about baseball emerge: Cuba produces a surplus of players, and the United States does not produce enough quality players to fill out the rosters of thirty major league teams. The solution to both problems? Cuban players reentering U.S. professional baseball. When relations between the two countries improve, Cuba will become the number one source of foreign-born talent in U.S. professional baseball. The world's largest producer of baseball players outside of the United States will be reunited with the world's largest consumer of baseball.

Statistics provided by the baseball industry show that almost 35 percent of players in professional baseball at all levels, from rookie to big league, were born outside of the United States. (Puerto Rico is included in this figure.) Baseball clearly is no longer just a U.S. sport;

it is an international one that is played at its highest level in the United States.

But Why Cuba?

Although Cubans really only had access to the major leagues between 1947 and 1960, 135 Cubans have played in the big leagues. Before 1947, only light-skinned Cubans were allowed to play; after 1960, only defectors. One can only imagine how many players from this baseball-crazy island would have reached the pinnacle of baseball had barriers not been in place.

Cuba's best athletes still choose baseball, and the Cuban people's deep love and understanding of the game permeate the island and ensure that baseball will continue with succeeding generations. These facts, coupled with Cuba's creation of a very effective system for identifying and developing young players, guarantees that Major League Baseball will keep its attention focused on the island. For all its defects, the Cuban political system after 1959 greatly expanded educational opportunities and availability of health care. The result is a more literate and healthier population than that of the Dominican Republic, which is currently the leading foreign supplier of players to the baseball industry in the United States.

"Cuban baseball today is at a crossroads—*está en 3 y 2*. It is facing a full count," Gilberto Dihigo, a Cuban baseball journalist whose father, Martín Dihigo, is enshrined at Cooperstown, told me. "Baseball will never die in Cuba, but it needs to be renovated." What is it about Cuba's baseball system that needs to be overhauled? Dihigo remembers an interview in the early 1980s with Carlos Rafael Rodríguez, the third-highest-ranking Cuban government official and clearly the Cuban leader who best understood the United States. Rodríguez, who died in late 1997, told Dihigo, "If you want to learn about technological development in baseball and the latest strategy, you have to talk with people in the United States. You have to give credit where credit is due." Cuban baseball officials understand this fact, even if the country's top political leaders are unwilling or unable to deal with it. *Es parte de la bronca.*

The image of Liván Hernández standing on the mound before the opening game of the 1997 World Series and the fact that it was seen, even if only on videotape, in Cuba ensures that young Cuban players will continue to dream about going to the United States. And the $312,042 share earned by Orlando "El Duque" Hernández for playing in the 1998 World Series means that winning the gold medal in the Olympics may no longer be as satisfactory a reward—especially given the economic hardship players must endure in Cuba.

Even so, there is something less tangible and more romantic about baseball in Cuba. One evening, I went to the Estadio Latinoamericano at 6:00 P.M. for a 7:30 P.M. game. Most of the Industriales players were standing around in the parking lot just outside the entrance to the ballpark. Dressed in their uniform pants and T-shirts, they were intently watching a serious game of street baseball being played by men between the ages of eighteen and thirty-five. There was no field or baselines, and there were only pieces of cardboard to mark the bases. No one hounded the Industriales players for autographs, and everyone was focused on the batter. With the sun setting on a beautiful winter afternoon in Havana, with Cuba's best players mingling with pick-up players, it was baseball at its best, harking back to images of the game long past in the United States.

2 ☆ "It Begins with the Dreams of Their Fathers": Baseball and National Identity in Cuba

In early 1997, I went to Havana with Tim Wendel, a writer for *USA Today Baseball Weekly*, to investigate the state of baseball on the island. Two hours after our plane landed, we were in the Estadio Latino-americano watching one of Havana's two teams, the Metropolitanos, play the team from the province of Las Tunas. I ran into Miguel Valdés in the stands just behind the backstop. We had visited before on several occasions over the past six years, both in Cuba and in the United States. I mentioned that we wanted to talk with Cuba's star third baseman, Omar Linares. Cubans joke that the country has only one boxer, 1960s Olympic gold medalist Teófilo Stevenson; one ballet dancer, Alicia Alonso; one leader, Fidel Castro; and one baseball player, Omar Linares. If there is one Cuban player U.S. baseball fans know anything about, it is Linares—clearly the best baseball player in the world who is not in the major leagues.

"That'll be difficult because Omar's team, Pinar del Río, is playing in Guantánamo the rest of the week," Valdés explained. Guantánamo is a fourteen-hour bus ride from Havana, and a trip was clearly out of the question. Then Valdés remembered that because Linares was injured, he was not traveling with the team and would be at home in Pinar del Río. As I wondered how we would get to Pinar del Río, Valdés volunteered, "You know, Omar will be at an awards ceremony tomorrow here in Havana, *la premiación del atleta del año 1996.* The ceremony starts at 11:00, at the Escuela de Medicina Victoria de Girón near the

13

Palacio de Convenciones in Miramar. If you are there by 10:30, you will be able to talk with him. He won't stay around long after the event is over," said Valdés.

The next morning Tim and I drove up to the security gate at the medical school, explained to the guard that we'd been invited to the awards ceremony and, to my surprise, were warmly greeted then told where to park. As we entered the school, we had no problem getting into what was a gathering of Cuba's best athletes. All of Cuba's gold medal winners from the Atlanta Olympics were to be honored. Inside, the four sides of an open patio were flanked by a couple of dozen school-children in uniforms, workers from the medical school, Cuban sports officials, and the more than thirty athletes receiving awards. On the balconies above, students, doctors, and military personnel looked down on the festivities. We joined a group of Cuban journalists as a government official explained the ground rules for covering the ceremony. I don't believe any foreign journalists had ever attended this annual event.

The sense of pride in the nation was palpable in the applause given each athlete, especially boxer Félix Savón and runner Ana Fidelia Quirot. But the loudest ovation was reserved for Omar Linares, giving credence to the interviews in which Linares and other Cuban baseball players have spoken of playing for the love of their country. After the ceremony, we spoke briefly with Linares, questioning him about the possibility of facing U.S. major leaguers. "It would be a series worth waiting for," he said. "We would get a chance to show how good a team we are."

Gilberto Dihigo: Son of "El Inmortal"

While some of the country's best athletes compete in basketball, volleyball, track and field, or boxing, the majority of the males clearly are steered into baseball. This tracking begins very early in life. At birth, boys quite often have a baseball glove placed over their crib. Miguel Valdés believes the focus on baseball starts even earlier. "It begins," he says, "with the dreams of their fathers." But where did their fathers get the dream? Where does this love of baseball originate?

Gilberto Dihigo knows. He is a Cuban sportswriter and passionate follower of baseball who inherited the dream from his father, Martín Dihigo, the only Cuban in the National Baseball Hall of Fame in Cooperstown, New York. Also honored in halls of fame in Mexico,

Cuba, and Venezuela, Martín Dihigo is considered one of the best baseball players in the history of the game.[1] In Cuba, he is known as "El Inmortal."

"Martín Dihigo was the best shortstop in Cuba. He was also the best pitcher. And when he played second base, he was the best. No one could top him in center field. He even caught," veteran Cuban sports writer Severo Nieto, who saw Dihigo play at the height of his career, explains. "The most remarkable trait Dihigo had as a baseball player was his uncanny versatility," writes Roberto González Echevarría in his epic work on Cuban baseball, *The Pride of Havana: A History of Cuban Baseball*. Dihigo played in Cuba, Mexico, and the U.S. Negro Leagues. "He was batting champion and leading pitcher in the same season twice, once in Cuba and another in Mexico."[2]

Martín Dihigo reportedly met Cuban revolutionary leader Ernesto "Che" Guevara in Mexico City in the early 1950s and gave financial support to the *Granma* expedition in 1956, which led to the victory of the forces led by Guevara and Fidel Castro in 1959. Later, Martín Dihigo returned to Cuba as a baseball instructor for the new Castro government. Gilberto Dihigo is in every sense a son of the Revolution— and of baseball.[3]

Gilberto, who now lives in Mexico, is a slim man in his mid-forties. While not a dissident in the sense that he actively works against the Cuban government, he is openly critical of Cuban governmental policies, especially those concerning baseball. And although Martín Dihigo is almost a mythic figure in Cuban baseball, Gilberto is very self-confident and seems not to be overwhelmed by his father's fame.

"Cuba is identified with sugar cane, tobacco, music, and baseball— in no particular order. These are the four essential elements which define Cuba," says Dihigo, between games of the Caribbean Series in Hermosillo, Mexico, in 1997. "Baseball is the national sport of Cuba, and baseball is part of the *nacionalidad cubana* [Cuban national identity]."

"When baseball began in Cuba [in the 1860s], it was a way of distinguishing between the Spanish, and the *criollos*, the children of Spaniards born in Cuba, who at this time still did not have a true identity," says Dihigo. "Baseball was a form of opposition to the ideas of Spain: to play baseball was to be *criollo*, to be *criollo* was to be Cuban."[4]

"Baseball was not played by the Spanish. They called it 'a rebel game.' To a certain point they were correct, because baseball players used the opportunity to collect money for the fight for independence from Spain," explains Dihigo. "Baseball was a meeting place for the rebels. Emilio Sabourín, who is one of the founders of Cuban baseball, was a prisoner of Spain in Ceuta [a Spanish prison in North Africa] for his role in the independence struggle. And there is a long list of baseball players who died fighting for the independence of Cuba. Baseball clearly distinguished Spaniards from Cubans, and this is where the Cuban love of baseball begins."[5]

Another important factor in the appeal of baseball to Cubans was that baseball came from the United States. "Cubans celebrated the modernity and progress implied in baseball, associated with the United States, and denounced the inhumanity and backwardness suggested by bullfighting, associated with Spain," writes historian Louis A. Pérez, Jr.[6]

And while baseball began as a game of middle- and upper-class Cubans, it quickly spread. It soon became an avenue for social advancement, immensely popular with all social classes and in all regions of the island. It has remained so for well over one hundred years.

The Cubans Start the Ball Rolling

As Dihigo points out, baseball was brought to Cuba in the 1860s. Nemesio Guilló, a Cuban who studied in the United States, is widely believed to have brought the first bat and baseball to Cuba in 1864. Guilló is variously described as the founder or the father of Cuban baseball.[7]

"I was a close friend of Alfonso Guilló, Nemesio's nephew," says Severo Nieto, who started writing about sports sixty years ago at the age of fifteen. "In 1943 or 1944 we worked together in the Ministerio de Obras Públicas [Ministry of Public Works]. He told me that his uncle brought the bat and ball to Cuba in 1864."

Nieto, who went to Havana in 1932 from his birthplace in Pinar del Río, is a wonderfully warm and generous person. He loves baseball and is anxious to share his interest and knowledge of the game with others. For most of the 1950s, Nieto worked for a daily newspaper, *Prensa Libre*, and after the Revolution in 1959, he wrote for the official government news agency, Prensa Latina, until his retirement in 1987.

On a previous trip, Nieto had brought part of his extensive collection of photographs to my hotel. This time I went to his small apartment just east of the famous stairs leading to the entrance of the University of Havana. His home is packed with sixty years of baseball writing and mementos, stamp and coin collections, and his granddaughter's toys.

I told Nieto I wanted to know more about Nemesio Guilló. I knew that Nieto was very organized, and I thought he might have the information tucked away in a old notebook. I was shocked when this elderly gentleman led me through the labyrinth of his apartment to a small desk surrounded by dolls. Making our way to his makeshift office was like walking through a tunnel. Nieto turned on his computer, pulled up his files on baseball, and after a few seconds displayed a biography of Guilló. After fifty-five years of working on a typewriter, Nieto began transferring more than half a century of research on Cuban baseball onto floppy disks when he was seventy years old.

"Guilló played in the first professional game in Havana, Habana versus Matanzas, in 1878. He was in right field for Habana. Bellán played in that game also," said Nieto, reading from the screen. (Estéban Bellán was the first Latin American to play in U.S. professional baseball.) I also learned that Guilló was right-handed, also played second base, and was inducted to the Cuban Hall of Fame in 1939. Nemesio and his brother Ernesto played with the Habana Base Ball Club, and both were on the first *junta directiva* (board of directors) of the club. Guilló was a regular with the Habana B.B.C. for several years between 1874 and 1880. From there he went to the Club Ultimatum in Havana. After his playing days, he turned to umpiring and then worked in the front office of the Habana B.B.C. By trade, Nemesio Guilló was an accountant.

Almost all sources agree that Guilló brought the first ball and bat to Cuba. After that, the information is less certain. Nieto has a note in his files listing Guilló as being born in 1847 and going to the United States in 1858. This same note lists his sibling Ernesto Guilló's year of birth as 1845 and states that the two brothers, along with another friend, went to Mobile, Alabama, to attend Springhill College. The date of death for Nemesio is recorded as September 27, 1931, at the age of eighty-four. In another file, Nieto has Guilló's date of death as October 1, 1935. He says he is not sure which date is correct. González Echevarría confirms the above facts about Guilló (although he does not give a date of death).

In 1868, Nemesio and Ernesto Guilló were among the founders of the Habana Base Ball Club. "It was in that year that the club first traveled to Matanzas, where Guilló remembers they played and defeated the crew of an American schooner anchored at that port for repairs," writes González Echevarría, drawing from an interview with Nemesio Guilló that was published in Cuba in 1924.[8]

Baseball's popularity spread quickly.[9] In 1872, the Habana Base Ball Club became the first professional team on the island, followed by the Matanzas club formed in 1874. In 1874, Cubans built their first baseball stadium, Palmar de Junco, in Matanzas, about sixty miles east of Havana. That same year, the stadium was the site of the first professional game in Cuba, between Matanzas and the Habana Base Ball Club. In 1878, the Almendares Base Ball Club was formed and, later that year, there was an organized professional baseball championship.

Baseball became a professional sport very early in Cuba because it was necessary to pay players from working-class backgrounds who otherwise would not have competed. But amateur baseball existed alongside the professional game in Cuba and, for many years, some outstanding Cuban players did not join the professional ranks. Many of these young men were in the leagues organized around Cuba's sugar mills, where they were given full-time employment, subsidized housing, and time off to play baseball. In the 1940s and 1950s, however, the possibility of playing professionally in Cuba in the winter and in either Cuba or the United States in the summer, coupled with difficult economic conditions, attracted the majority of Cuba's best players to the professional ranks.

The first game between U.S. and Cuban clubs was played in Havana in 1878—between a local team, Almendares, and the Hops Bitter team from Massachusetts. (Nieto also refers to this team as Worcester).[10] In the winter of 1890, the New York Giants traveled to Havana. The Brooklyn Dodgers played the New York Giants in exhibition games in Havana in 1900, and the Brooklyn team also played against a Cuban all-star team on the same trip.[11] The New York Giants held spring training in Havana in 1937. The Dodgers trained in Havana in 1941 and 1942, and returned to Havana in 1947 to conduct spring training, in order to provide Jackie Robinson a more relaxed and less segregated atmosphere than Florida.[12]

Today, baseball completely dominates all other sports on the island. Soccer, a passion throughout most of Latin America, is so rare in Cuba that U.S. intelligence sources could detect the presence of Soviet sailors in Cuba in 1971 through satellite images of a soccer field. "Our people place some significance on the fact that a soccer field was built there . . . because soccer is not a sport that is common to Cuba. . . . You would expect to find baseball diamonds," Colonel John Bridge, head of the Soviet Area Office of the Defense Intelligence Agency, told a committee of the U.S. House of Representatives in 1971.[13]

Cuba Exports Baseball

While many in the United States assume baseball was taken to Venezuela, the Dominican Republic, Puerto Rico, and Mexico during one of the early U.S. interventions or occupations in the region, it was in fact Cubans who introduced baseball to neighboring countries.

"In the Dominican Republic, Cubans who had migrated to escape the turmoil of the Ten Years War (1868–1878) were the first to form teams," writes Rob Ruck in *The Tropic of Baseball*. "Young Dominicans emulated them and joined with compatriots who had studied in the United States to establish a self-organized matrix of teams and tournaments well in place before the U.S. Marines arrived in 1916 for their eight-year occupation."[14]

"Continued violent struggles against colonial Spain caused many Cubans to flee the island, settling in Puerto Rico and the Dominican Republic," notes historian Adrian Burgos. "This Cuban migration led to the game's further spread and blurred national identities since many migrants never returned."[15]

Baseball was introduced to Venezuela in the mid-1890s, again with the aid of Cubans. Havana cigar manufacturer Emilio Cramer established La Cubana cigarette factory in Caracas and, along with other Cuban immigrants and locals, put together a five-team league in the city.[16] "Led by Cramer, Cuban émigrés in Caracas organized the Carlos Manuel de Céspedes Baseball Club (named for a hero of the Ten Years' War), an all-star team that played exhibition games for the express purpose of raising revenues." Money earned was used to fight for Cuba's independence from Spain.[17]

Cubans also took baseball to the Gulf Coast and Caribbean regions of Mexico in the 1890s. "Fleeing the turbulence of their homeland during the war for independence from Spain," writes historian Gilbert Joseph, "many Cubans sought a haven in neighboring Yucatán, bringing their passion for the game with them. . . . It is not surprising, therefore, that many early Yucatecan ball clubs proudly carried such names as 'Habana,' 'Matanzas,' or 'Cuba.'"[18]

Cuban Players in the United States

In 1871, Cuban Estéban Bellán became the first Latino to play professional baseball in the United States, with a team in Troy, New York. The first Cubans to play in the major leagues were Rafael Almeida and Armando Marsans with the Cincinnati Reds in 1911.[19] The most successful and popular Cuban of this early period was Adolfo Luque, a pitcher with the Cincinnati Reds in the 1920s.[20]

"Because of Adolfo Luque, Cincinnati in the 1920s was the favorite team in Cuba," explains Gilberto Dihigo.[21] "If you read the Cuban newspapers from this period you will see expressions like *nuestros queridos Reds* [our beloved Reds], or *querido Cinci*, as if Cincinnati were a region of Cuba." *Granma* writer Sigfredo Barros says that the expression *querido Cinci* is still used in Cuba today.

A total of 39 Cubans had made it to the big leagues by 1946. In the early 1940s, the Washington Senators and the first regional super scout, Joe Cambria, recruited Cubans to fill out rosters decimated because U.S. players were pressed into military service during World War II. Between 1947 and 1959, when Fidel Castro took power, Cubans were the major source of Latin talent for the majors. From Orestes "Minnie" Miñoso to Tony Oliva and Tony Peréz, Cubans were a vital part of U.S. professional baseball.

Before Jackie Robinson broke the color barrier in 1947, opportunities for Cuban players in the United States, most of whom were black, were limited. Many of Cuba's stars played in the U.S. Negro Leagues, including Martín Dihigo.[22] The 1936 New York Cubans featured Dihigo, Manuel "Cocaína" García,[23] Lázaro Salazar, and Luis Tiant, Sr., all among the greatest ever to play Cuban baseball.[24] A few black Cubans played only on barnstorming tours of the United States. One of these players was Santos Amaro. Amaro is extremely proud of his forty-year career as a player and manager in Mexico, Cuba, Venezuela, and the Dominican Republic. He is considered one of the best hitters in the history of the Mexican League, where he had a career average of .314.

But almost a decade after Jackie Robinson opened the door, dark-skinned Cuban players still suffered from the overt racism of the U.S.

South. "When I moved to Texas it was tough, because I could not live with the other players on the club, even though I was the hero," remembers Rubén Amaro, Santos's son. "I was the All-Star shortstop, and I won the Dixie Series with a home run in the sixth game against Atlanta." But being black in Texas in the 1950s meant Rubén couldn't go out to dinner to celebrate with his teammates. And Fidel Castro took power in 1959 before the Boston Red Sox had their first black player, Pumpsie Green.

Professional Baseball in Cuba: A Visit with Edel Casas

During a 1992 visit to Cuba, I was to be a guest on *Deportivamente*, the nightly sports talk show on Radio Rebelde. Radio Rebelde started in 1958 as the clandestine station of Castro's Rebel Army operating in the Sierra Maestra. It relocated to Havana in 1959 and occupied the studios of what had been the official radio station of dictator Fulgencio Batista. When I arrived at the studio, I found I had been bumped by a broadcast of a women's volleyball game.

"I'm sorry you won't be on the show, but I want you to meet a man who works with us and knows everything about U.S. baseball," Roberto Pacheco, one of the hosts of *Deportivamente*, told me as I arrived. He introduced me to Edel Casas. Casas appeared younger than I would have expected—probably about sixty-five. He explained that he had never been to the United States and had never seen a major league game. Casas, fascinated by Major League Baseball as a kid, has seemingly memorized the *Baseball Encyclopedia*. He can tell you who won the batting title in the American League in 1941, who won the Cy Young Award in 1961, and a million other facts about Major League Baseball.

"No American trivia expert could surpass Casas on the genuinely trivial," baseball writer Thomas Boswell noted in 1982.[25] When I read Boswell's comments, I pictured a sort of court jester of baseball information. But Casas is no joke; he is the island's king of information about baseball. I explained to Casas that, with all due respect, I was not interested in talking about Ted Williams or Whitey Ford but instead wanted to know about baseball in Cuba. Casas seemed relieved and proceeded to talk for over two hours.

Casas explained that the first Cuban professional leagues were organized in 1878, twenty years before Cuba gained its independence from Spain, and that Cuba was the second country in the world after the United States to play a championship series in baseball. Before being abolished in 1961, professional baseball was played in Cuba for over eighty years. Although Habana won the most championships, Casas thought Almendares—another Havana-based club—was the most popular club. "The loyalty to these teams was fierce," explained Casas. "You got attached to one team or another, and it could split families."

Casas fast-forwarded to the mid-1940s, when Habana and Almendares were joined by two other Havana-based clubs: Marianao and Cienfuegos. "The teams all played in the same stadium, so they all saw each other. They played on Tuesday, Wednesday, Thursday, off Friday and Saturday, a doubleheader on Sunday and off Monday," said Casas, as if talking about something happening this week, not a ritual that ended thirty years earlier.

The four Cuban teams were reinforced by imports from the United States. Among Casas's favorite import players were Jim Bunning, now a U.S senator, and Bill Virdon, former manager and coach with the Houston Astros. Virdon played in Cuba only once, with the Habana team during the 1954–55 winter season, and went on to become Rookie of the Year in the National League in 1955.

"It was between my Triple A and my first major league year. I had a good year at Rochester, and they [the St. Louis Cardinals] asked me if I would like to go and play winter ball," recalled Virdon before an Astros game in 1997. "There was no travel, and we played every other day—ideal for winter ball. I don't know how you would have a better situation than we had that particular winter. The quality of play was definitely better than Triple A level, and the Cuban fans were excellent. They like baseball."

Winter baseball in Cuba provided an opportunity for the country's best players to compete with the U.S. major leaguers and afforded Cuban fans the chance to see top-quality baseball. The last winter ball season was 1960–61.

"In 1946, a summer league started that was sanctioned by the National Association of Professional Baseball Leagues [the governing body of the U.S. minor leagues]," Casas told me. "The Havana Cubans—with only Cuban players—played in the league that included teams in Miami, Fort Lauderdale, West Palm Beach, and Tampa. The Cuban team won the title all five years they played in league."

Actually, the Havana Cubans won the first five titles of the Florida International League between 1946 and 1950. The circuit, which varied between six and eight franchises, was Class C for the first four years and was then upgraded to Class B after the 1948 season. The Havana team finished in fourth or fifth place between 1951 and 1953. It did not field a team in 1954, the year in which the league folded before the end of the season.[26]

Between 1956 and 1960, Havana had a team—the Cuban Sugar Kings—in the AAA International League.[27] The franchise was transferred to Jersey City in July 1960, marking an end to professional baseball in Cuba. The unthinkable came to pass when Fidel Castro abolished the professional game on the island in 1961.

Havana Monuments to Life, Death, and Baseball

There are two little-known monuments to professional baseball in Havana: one is on the southeast corner of H and 9th in Vedado, behind the Hospital Materno América Arias (better known as Maternidad de Línea), where most of Havana's children are born; the other is in the Cementerio Colón, where 70 percent of all burials in Havana take place.

The monument near the hospital, erected in 1953 on the centenary of Emilio Sabourín's birth, is located on the former site of the stadium where Havana's first professional game was played in 1878. The monument has a bust of Sabourín, honoring him for his contributions to Cuba and to baseball, and an inscription describing him as a patriot, revolutionary, baseball pioneer, and founder of the Club Habana, a 21–20 winner over the Almendares Base Ball Club in that first contest.

Cuban friends had told me about a monument to baseball players at Havana's enormous Cementerio Colón. I'm not sure what I expected, but the bust of Emilio Sabourín set atop one of the crypts is rather unimpressive. A plaque explains that this section of the cemetery belonged to the Asociación Cristiana de Players, Umpires y Managers de Baseball Profesional. Sabourín is not buried there; nor are most famous Cuban players.

Edith Monterde, whose official title is Especialista Principal, Equipo Técnico Necrópolis Cristóbal Colón, graciously met me in her office in the administrative building near the main entrance. She is an expert on the cemetery's history and explained that it is very difficult to say precisely who is buried in any of the crypts. Each property is in the hands of the owners, and the cemetery does not have all of the records. When the cemetery and the funeral homes in Cuba were nationalized in 1960, however, some property titles were given to the cemetery.

Given those limitations, she was happy to answer any questions I might have and sent her assistant out to determine whether official records of the baseball tract were available. In a few minutes, the assistant returned with a large book in which the names of all those buried in the section belonging to the players association were listed.

"This property was transferred to INDER [Instituto Nacional de Deporte, Educación Física y Recreación] in 1992, because the association that owned it no longer exists," explained Monterde. She let me examine the original record books with the names and dates of burials carefully handwritten in the ledgers. The first burial was in 1944, the last in 1993. There were fifty players buried in the section. The only player who appeared in the major leagues was Armando Marsans—the first Cuban in the big leagues—an outfielder with Cincinnati, the St. Louis Browns, and the New York Yankees between 1911 and 1918. Born in Matanzas in 1887, Marsans died in Havana in 1960. In a way, the monument is one to professional baseball in Cuba, which died less than one year later.

Fidel and Cuban Baseball

What are the chances of Cuban players signing professional contracts in the future? Casas shrugged his shoulders, "It is possible," he said. "But only Fidel can make it happen."

In Cuba, President Fidel Castro is almost omnipotent. For the past forty years, Fidel has overshadowed almost every aspect of Cuban life and, of course, he is intimately tied to Cuban baseball. It was his policy that eliminated professional baseball in 1961, and it is from his regime that players defect today.

And was Fidel Castro ever really a baseball prospect? Was he really offered a contract? Rumors abound about both. "What about Fidel and baseball?" I asked. "Joe Cambria of the Washington Senators met with Fidel in 1942 or 1943, when Fidel was 16 or 17. He was a right-handed pitcher and was offered a contract by Cambria," explained Casas. "Fidel turned him down, but no one knows what his best pitch was because he never pitched in organized baseball in an organized league." Castro told International Baseball Association president Robert Smith in 1987 that while he had a good arm, he didn't know the technique of pitching. "Even so, the scout wanted to sign me, but I refused."[28]

Others remember Castro's flirtation with professional baseball differently. "Cambria even turned down Fidel Castro twice," Rubén Amaro told writer Kevin Kerrane. "He could have changed history if he remembered that some pitchers just mature late."[29]

An article by J. David Truby reprinted in *Harper's Magazine* in 1989 describes four scouting reports on Castro. "We had our top people evaluate him, as did several other teams. Castro was a real prospect," New York Giants owner Horace C. Stoneham is reported to have commented. "He was a good prospect because he could throw and think at the same time, a rare talent in a young pitcher," says long-time Latin market scout Howie Haak. According to Truby, Cambria is reported to have been impressed with Castro. "Fidel Castro is a big, powerful young man. His fastball is not great, but passable. He uses good curve variety. He uses his head and can win that way for us too." New York Giants scout Alex Pompez reported in 1948 that Castro "has good control and should be considered seriously." Pompez, reports Truby, "offered Castro a $5,000 signing bonus, and was stunned when the offer was turned down."[30]

Tad Szulc writes that Castro "forcefully denied a rumor then circulating abroad that he had once hoped to play for the majors in mainland baseball."[31] He does point out that Castro was an outstanding athlete in high school and was a pitcher on the baseball team.

I asked Casas about Don Hoak's 1964 article in *Sport* in which Hoak claims Fidel came on to the field during a student protest in 1951 or 1952 and took the mound. Casas says this claim is completely false. He remembers Don Hoak playing third base for Cienfuegos in the 1950s. He says that José Antonio Echevarría, president of the student association, might have gone to the mound during a game.[32]

Baseball historian Peter Bjarkman has thoroughly investigated the Hoak story and has concluded that it is a fictional account. Nonetheless, for many in the United States, it remains the cornerstone of the belief that Fidel was actually a baseball prospect.[33]

Fidel's obsession with baseball places intense pressure on the coaching staff of Cuba's national team. "I'm talking about the politicians, such as the first secretary of the Communist Party who calls the manager and wants to know why they are not winning," explains Gilberto Dihigo. "They are like the club owners. And, of course, the big club owner is Fidel Castro."

"Fidel often meets with the players," Dihigo continues. "When I came back from Puerto Rico with the team in 1989, we arrived in the very early morning and went to the palace and met with Fidel. And Fidel watches all of the games. And then he says to an aide, 'Why did they do this?' or 'Why did they do that?'"

Fidel: "He Always Had Great Control"

As I stood in Havana's Parque Central in early 1997, a man walked by with a small bundle of newspapers. I had never seen anyone selling newspapers (they are usually sold out by early morning), so I asked him where I could buy one. "I sell them, " said Sigfredo Medina. I gave him a five-peso bill (about twenty-five cents U.S.), for which he had no change. I asked if he liked baseball. "I'm an Industriales fan, but the quality of play has diminished. Rey Ordóñez left and Germán Mesa had his problem. Mesa is the best shortstop to ever play in Cuba."

Medina is sixty-nine, lives on a pension of 170 pesos a month (approximately $7.50 U.S.), and makes another 20 pesos selling newspapers, an occupation which he uses as an opportunity to visit with old friends and make new acquaintances. "I'm doing well," he said. "I have relatives who live in Dayton, Ohio, and they want me to go, but I don't want to live in cold weather."

Medina, from a small town in eastern Cuba, explained that when he was sixteen, in 1943, he went to the equivalent of high school in the regional capital of Santiago. "I played first base for my school and Fidel played first base for the other team," said Medina. Fidel as in Fidel Castro I asked? "Yes," Medina replied matter-of-factly. I asked if he ever talked with Fidel back then? "Sure, we would play catch before the games." Did he ever see Fidel these days? "No," as he made a motion with his hand indicating that the *comandante en jefe* (commander-in-chief) was busy with other things.

"Even though he played first base, Fidel was really a pitcher," said Medina. I was intrigued because I knew no one who had actually seen Fidel pitch. What were Fidel's best pitches, I asked?

"He was kind of like "El Duque" [Orlando Hernández], the guy who just got banned. He had a great curve ball on the outside corner.

And a low breaking ball that came in on the knees," Medina said. "And he had great control. He always had great control."

"When he learned to play baseball, he always insisted on pitching. If he lost or played poorly, he quit and went home, taking all the equipment. It belonged to him," writes Robert Quirk in his biography on Castro.[34] But as is evident, neither baseball, nor Cuba, belongs to Fidel Castro. Baseball in Cuba has a long tradition that predates Castro: Cuba, in fact, won the first championship of the Central American Games in 1926, the year Fidel was born.[35]

In the mid-1980s, Italian journalist Gianni Miná asked Fidel to explain where Cuba's passion for baseball came from. "Really we should have played soccer, because we were a Spanish colony. And the Spanish didn't play baseball, they played soccer. I believe it is the result of North American influence and the prestige of the Major Leagues, *la gran publicidad*,"[36] answered Castro, never mentioning the role played by baseball in organizing to defeat the Spanish and bring about Cuban independence.

And when talking to a Cable News Network reporter in 1996, Castro said: "It's an American legacy. It's a good thing that the Americans left off."[37] But baseball in Cuba is far more than an "American legacy." "Baseball is so ingrained in Cuba that it has thrived as 'the national sport' through forty years of a bitterly anti-American revolution," writes González Echevarría. "The coincidence of the birth of the nation and the inception of the game is a key in understanding that resiliency."[38]

The strong roots of baseball on the island are reflected in the ever present discussion of baseball, the kids playing on the streets, and the young players that continue to emerge. No matter how seriously the current baseball system is in crisis, Cuba continues to produce world-class players, and the love of the game continues to be reproduced in the younger generation.

In the late nineteenth century, Cubans used baseball as a vehicle to project a more important message: national identity. Fidel, like the Cubans fighting for independence against Spain, would also use baseball; only this time, he would try to use the "American game" as a weapon against a different enemy: the United States. Clearly Fidel understood that baseball is much more than an "American legacy": it is at the core of being Cuban."One day, when the Yankees accept peaceful coexistence with our own country," said Fidel in a 1974 speech, "we shall beat them at baseball too and then the advantages of revolutionary over capitalist sport will be shown."[39]

Shortly after the victory of the Cuban Revolution in 1959, professional baseball was abolished, and *béisbol revolucionario* was inaugurated. With all of the talent confined to the island, the new regime could begin the process of assembling the best amateur baseball team in the world. For the past thirty-eight years, the Cubans have played only amateur baseball—dominating all international competitions, winning the first Olympic gold medal in the sport in Barcelona in 1992, and capturing the gold again in Atlanta in 1996.

3 ☆ *Béisbol Revolucionario:* The Best Amateur Baseball in the World

When the government abolished all professional sports on the island in 1960, viewing them as counter to the principles of the Revolution, more than eighty years of Cuban professional baseball came to a halt. Selling baseball players, Fidel believed, was a crude manifestation of the worst elements of capitalism, akin to slavery, and he referred to professional baseball as *la pelota esclava*. For Fidel, the first Serie Nacional in 1961–1962 was *el triunfo de la pelota libre sobre la pelota esclava* (the triumph of free baseball over slave baseball).[1]

Each time I saw *equipo Cuba*, I was impressed with the talent level, the discipline, and how professionally the players handled themselves. I asked Edel Casas how he defined the term *professional*. "A professional plays the game at a very high level and always conducts himself in a responsible manner," Casas replied. Why then, since they clearly met this definition, were Cuban baseball players not considered professional? "In terms of quality, the Cuban team is professional," said Casas, and after pausing for a moment added, *"Pero chico, no ganan* [But man, they don't get paid]."

The rivalry between Habana and Almendares, which began in the 1870s, lasted until 1961 when both teams ceased to exist. From conversations with older fans in Havana, the best way to describe the games between these two Havana teams is like those between the Brooklyn

Dodgers and the New York Giants in the 1940s and 1950s. "*Béisbol revolucionario* begins with new players, and with new teams. Instead of Habana and Almendares, we have the Industriales and a team from Oriente (eastern Cuba). The rivalry of Habana and Almendares is replaced by renewing the old antagonism of the people of the Oriente—principally Santiago de Cuba—and Havana," explained Dihigo. "When Santiago de Cuba and a team from Havana play, *olvídese usted* [forget it], this is Santiago against Havana, *no hay otra* [there is nothing like it]. This competition brings the antagonism between eastern and western Cuba to a fever pitch. The only way to deal with this practically, without going to war, was through baseball. Baseball is converted into a catharsis to express these regional differences."

For the first four years of *béisbol revolucionario*, there were only four teams. In 1965, the number of teams was expanded to six, and in 1967 to twelve. Even though attendance remained high, fans were not very enthusiastic about the new setup. That changed in the 1970s when the government placed teams in each of Cuba's newly created fourteen provinces and played even more upon regional rivalries to generate fan interest. By the mid-1970s, the new system was firmly in place: *béisbol revolucionario* was now totally consolidated and Cuban fans again became passionate about baseball.

But the transition was not easy. Fans were understandably reluctant to transfer their allegiance from one of the old professional teams to one in the newly created amateur leagues. With the coming of *béisbol revolucionario* in 1961, Dihigo explained, fans lost their *fetiches*, their emotional attachment with the old professional teams. They had to look for new *fetiches*, and from time to time they found them in the players. Today that player is Omar Linares.

Omar Linares: The Best Amateur Baseball Player in the World

San Juan y Martínez, in the western province of Pinar del Río, produces the highest quality tobacco in Cuba. It is also home to the player that many feel is the island's all-time best, Omar Linares. When he was fourteen, in 1981, Linares was on the team representing Cuba at the world junior championships in Venezuela, a competition usually limited to players in the sixteen- to eighteen-year-old range. Three years later, at age seventeen, he made his first trip with *equipo Cuba* to the Intercontinental Cup in Canada, and earned his nickname *El Niño* (the kid). By the time he was eighteen, he was already considered the world's best third baseman in amateur baseball. In Cuba, singling out players as stars is discouraged, but Linares broke the mold and he is unquestionably the *fetiche* of Cuban baseball.

I had the opportunity to see Linares play and to speak with him on several occasions in both Cuba and the United States between 1991 and 1999. He is very low-key, self-assured, and confident, but not cocky. He chooses his words carefully, but it's obvious that he would much rather be taking ground balls than talking to a reporter, especially one from the United States. Always courteous with the foreign press, he frequently gives stock answers to oft-repeated questions. Like other Cuban players, he understands that he has absolutely nothing to gain from granting interviews.

"I don't see myself as a hero, but as an expression of the youth of Cuba and what they can accomplish," Linares said in our first interview in 1991. "Baseball is so important in Cuba. The most important thing for a player is to be chosen to *equipo Cuba* to represent *nuestro Cuba*." Linares is sincere in his love for his country. In an age where the world's great athletes are viewed more as entertainers than as sports figures, Omar Linares is a rarity. He is a world-class athlete whom few fans know about. He is also an incredibly talented player who has turned down million-dollar opportunities to leave his country and play professional baseball, and those offers have been coming since he was seventeen. In 1985, the Toronto Blue Jays reportedly tendered him a contract to play only in home games in Canada, thus sidestepping the U.S. trade embargo.

"Omar Linares is the best amateur player in the world. He has all the tools. He is fast, a strong arm, power, and above all he has a great temperament for the game," said his manager Jorge Fuentes in 1991. A 1993 major league scouting report called Linares a "gifted, solid, everyday, front-line major league player."

"As with players like Ken Griffey, Jr. and Mo Vaughn, Linares has a magnetic presence just standing on the field. Raised in a system that taught him baseball as if it were history or math, he is like a scholar who uses his arm, speed and power to apply his knowledge," observed *Bos-*

ton *Globe* writer Steve Fainaru in 1995.[2] Out of uniform at the awards ceremony in 1997, Linares looked like a U.S. major league player walking out of a clubhouse after a game. In fact, since putting on additional weight, he resembles Tony Gwynn.

There are those—both in Miami and Havana—who will argue that Omar Linares is overrated. He hits a lot of home runs, they say, because he is committed to the communist government and they order the pitchers to put the ball over the plate for him to hit. But, even if he were hitting batting practice pitchers in Cuba (which he is not), why does Linares hit so well against pitchers from the U.S. Olympic team?

A Child of the Revolution

Linares often describes his decision to remain in Cuba, making the equivalent of $20 a month plus a few perks not available to the average Cuban, as based upon the gains that he and his family made through the Revolution. Linares is sometimes criticized in the United States for turning down millions to play professional baseball, but few understand what he would leave behind. "I have all of my family here, and the Revolution has given me everything. It has permitted me to study, to practice sports, and to reach the level I have reached," Linares told a CNN reporter in 1996. "I don't need to leave my country or the Revolution."[3]

Linares has obviously been influenced by his father, Fidel Linares, also a native of San Juan y Martínez. Fidel Linares left school in the third grade to work with his father in the tobacco fields. Like many other Cubans, he describes himself as *un enfermo a la pelota* (crazy about baseball). The elder Linares is also thankful that baseball and the Revolution gave him the opportunity to fulfill his dreams.[4]

Before 1959, Pinar del Río province in western Cuba was almost completely neglected by the Havana-dominated central government. Without much prompting, Cubans will tell you that Pinar del Río was the Cinderella of Cuba and will proudly list the improvements in the province after 1959. (Most Cubans are also quick to tell you a *pinareño* story—the Cuban equivalent of the ethnic joke.) Fidel Linares was lucky even to get an opportunity to play baseball, and he believes there is a very simple reason why not many players came from Pinar del Río before the Revolution: there were no stadiums with lights, there was no one scouting for players from the province, nor was there any effort given to develop the few who did emerge. He felt a responsibility to play well as a reminder to other Cubans that Pinar del Río was also baseball country.[5]

On January 14, 1961, thirty-year-old Fidel Linares, a left-handed hitting outfielder, saw his dream come true when he walked on the field at the Estadio Latinoamericano to play in the *Primera Serie Nacional* under the new amateur system. And for several years, he was the only well-known player from Pinar del Río province. Everyone in Pinar del Río knows and respects him, and whenever there is a baseball game, neighbors gather in front of his television set to watch and to complain about the umpires.[6] For the last few years, they have seen their Pinar del Río team become the dominant squad in the Cuban League, thanks in part to the outstanding play of Omar Linares. But Fidel Linares and his friends will never see Omar play in the major leagues, and their disappointment is shared by most Cubans. "I would love to see Omar Linares play in the big leagues," says Edel Casas, adding a comment heard throughout the island. "Until he plays there, he is not the best in baseball."

The Road to *Equipo Cuba:* The Best Amateur Baseball Team in the World

How is a young boy, possibly a future Omar Linares, with dreams of representing his country incorporated into Cuba's outstanding baseball program? I asked Miguel Valdés to describe the baseball recruitment process. He was reluctant, but consented after I explained that I would be using the information in a book, not in a newspaper article where his comments might be taken out of context. As in the case of the players, he has very little to gain and much to lose by talking to a reporter from the United States.

Valdés was, until late 1997, the *director técnico*—the person in charge of *equipo Cuba*. The "director," or manager, can change from year to year, but Valdés, as the combination general manager and director of player development, spent twenty-nine years with the team before being "reassigned" (demoted) after Cuba's loss in the Intercontinental Cup finals in Barcelona in August 1997. Valdés loved his job, and all who know him, both in and out of Cuba, respect him. But with the crisis in both Cuban baseball and the Cuban economy, "Miguelito," as he is known to most Cubans, came under increasing pressure. He played a major role in selecting *equipo Cuba*. When there was criticism of how the team was selected, who was selected, or who retired, Valdés was often blamed.

"The secret to the success of Cuban baseball is the large number of young men who play baseball," explained Valdés. He then described in detail the process that takes tens of thousands of dreams and converts a minuscule number of them into the twenty-four slots on *equipo Cuba*. He used the analogy of an inverted pyramid, or a funnel—wide at the top and very narrow at the bottom. I have heard the same comparison from several U.S. minor league farm directors when discussing a prospect's chances for success.

When students are age five, physical education instructors in primary schools evaluate the abilities of the youngsters and steer them toward various sports, although most boys choose baseball because they are encouraged to by their fathers. Those who elect baseball begin to learn the ABCs of the game. At age eight, they will begin to play in interschool tournaments. The entire baseball program from these early youth leagues through the selection of *equipo Cuba* is organized by the Instituto Nacional de Deportes, Educación Física y Recreación (National Institute of Sports, Physical Education, and Recreation)—INDER.[7] Created in 1961, INDER, borrowing heavily from Eastern European and Soviet models, is in charge of all sports in Cuba.

"When they are ten, the boys move into specialized areas where baseball *técnicos* begin to look for prospects," explained Valdés, utilizing the term *buscador de talento de béisbol* (baseball talent scout). "At this age we encourage them to just play baseball. Sometimes instructors make the mistake of trying to teach kids too much technique. And what happens is that the kid gets bored and quits playing baseball," said Valdés. Then he stopped to ponder the significance of what he had just said. "*Que bueno que le gusta jugar béisbol* [It's great he likes to play baseball]. Just let him play baseball."

Before the kids are age twelve, all of the games are designed to improve the relative speed of the players. "*Por qué?* [Why?]" asks Valdés rhetorically, in a fashion often used in Cuba. "Because we have found that it is difficult to improve on the speed [*frequencia del paso*] of a player after he is twelve or thirteen." At age thirteen, Cuba's best baseball prospects move on to the first of a two-tiered specialized sports education program.

TABLE 1

Cuba's Baseball Pyramid with Number of Players at Each Level

Equipo Cuba (24)

Cuba B (24)

Preselección (50)

Serie Nacional (400)

Group A	Group B	Group C	Group D
Pinar del Río	Provincia Habana	Villa Clara	Holguín
Isla de la Juventud	Industriales	Ciego de Ávila	Granma
Metropolitanos	Sancti Spíritus	Camagüey	Santiago de Cuba
Matanzas	Cienfuegos	Las Tunas	Guantánamo

Serie de Desarrollo (416)*

Group A	Group B	Group C	Group D
Vegueros	Agropecuarios	Azucareros	Mineros
Pescadores	Constructores	Agricultores	Cafetaleros
Capitalinos	Camaroneros	Granjeros	Serranos
Citricultores	Arroceros	Cañeros	Salineros

Escuela Superior de Perfeccionamiento Atlético (ESPA)
Fifteen schools with 850 players

Escuela de Iniciación Deportiva (EIDE)
Fifteen schools with 1,250 players

*Teams are listed according to cities in columns for Serie Nacional.

Escuela de Iniciación Deportiva
(Sports Initiation School)—EIDE

The care the Cubans take in developing young talent is in stark contrast to the way things were done before 1959. At that time, there was no systematic program to develop players, and the best young prospects were signed by U.S. professional teams. John Sugden, in his book on boxing, notes that the current Cuban system stands out even when compared to that of the United States or Ireland. "In Cuba . . . potential is recognized early and protected within special schools of excellence where, in the hands of well qualified coaches, talent can be maximized, with a single goal in mind—to produce amateur champions who will win international honors for Cuba."[8]

The best players go to Escuelas de Iniciación Deportiva (Sports Initiation Schools)—EIDE. These are special boarding schools where student athletes between ages thirteen and sixteen study half the day and practice the other half. There are fifteen of these schools located throughout Cuba. Wanting to visit an EIDE, I made a request to baseball commissioner Carlos Rodríguez, who arranged for one of his staff, Andrés Díaz, to take me to Cotorro, a forty-five minute drive south of Havana to see the EIDE for the Ciudad de La Habana.

My conversation with Díaz on the way to Cotorro was as fascinating as the visit to the school itself. It soon became apparent that Díaz knew Cuban baseball very well indeed. He works with all levels of baseball for youngsters between the ages of seven and sixteen. In fact, Díaz is in charge of these age-groups—collectively called *categoría escolar*— for the entire island. Díaz explained that players are divided into five age groups and that a national team that represents Cuba in international competitions is selected in each of the five categories beginning at age nine.

Baseball is organized by province, of which there are fourteen in Cuba, and then by *municipio* (roughly equivalent to a U.S. county); each *municipio* (there are 169 in Cuba) is broken down by neighborhood or barrio. For example, in the city of Havana alone, there are 15 *municipios*. There are teams at each level—barrio, *municipio*, and province—for ages nine through seventeen. A national championship is played at the provincial level in each of the age groups: 9–10, 11–12, 13–14, 15–16, and 17–18.

"We see players when they are very young. Their dream is to play on the national team in their age category," explains Díaz as we ride through the suburbs of Havana that abruptly become as rural as any place on the island. Díaz has been to every EIDE in Cuba. *"Yo conozco Cuba pedacito por pedacito* [I know Cuba piece by piece]," he tells me, with an expression that shows he remembers all of the miles and hours on buses and trains spent doing his job. He seldom travels by car and never by plane.

"I go wherever there is a player, or a place where they play baseball," says Díaz. He is so aware of the talent in Cuba that he can state unpretentiously, "If someone tells me there is a boy over ten who is a good player and I don't know his name, he is probably not a prospect." I ask him about a youngster from Villa Clara I saw in the nine- to ten-year-old game before the all-star game in Ciego de Ávila in 1998. He was tall, played first base, had a double in the game, and was wearing number 71.

"His name is Juan Yasser Serrano," Díaz says without hesitation. "He is ten and he will go to the *feria de béisbol infantil* [baseball youth fair] in Japan this summer. Serrano's team won the national championship in the nine-to-ten age-group." Serrano is one of five young players who went to Japan in 1998. Trips such as these are designed as a reward for a player's efforts and to keep the player loyal to the government.

Clearly, baseball talent is identified at an early age in Cuba. I recalled a segment on ABC's *Good Morning America* that aired when Pope John Paul II visited Cuba. Although there are baseball stadiums dotting the island, the ABC crew found a field with grass a foot high and grazing goats. Reporter Kevin Newman interviewed a young man, perhaps sixteen years old, playing baseball there. His dream, he told Newman, was to play on *equipo Cuba*. Both the young man and Newman smiled and the piece ended. A sixteen-year-old who has not been identified as a prospect has about as much chance of playing on *equipo Cuba* as a person singing in the New York subway has of being selected to join the Metropolitan Opera.

The EIDE we visited was the Mártires de Barbados. The best young sports prospects of the city of Havana are here, selected from the fifteen *municipios* of the city. At the EIDE, two thousand young men and women ranging in age from thirteen to sixteen study, play sports, and live at the school. About one hundred are in the baseball program.

"In another country, you would call me a scout, although they don't often use that term here in Cuba," said Díaz, age thirty-two, who is from the nearby town of Cuatro Caminos—the town that is also the home of Germán Mesa. Díaz, who resembles Philadelphia Phillies outfielder Bob Kelly Abreu, was the pitching coach for the Industriales for three years and worked with Orlando "El Duque" Hernández.

We arrive at the school in Cotorro, and because Díaz is the director of baseball at this level for the entire country and comes here once a month, I assumed we would be escorted in. We were not. "I'm Andrés Díaz, *director nacional de béisbol escolar* [national director of youth baseball], and I have a foreign journalist with me," he announced to the two women at the school's entrance gate. The words *foreign journalist* made the women freeze. I had encountered this type of person in Cuba before. Not too bright, expressionless, moves very slowly—and always keeps you from your mission. It is as if this type of person has been programmed and can only respond to some authority figure who is absent. In any event, the automatons called someone and we waited. Five minutes passed, and Díaz apologized for the delay. After another five minutes, Díaz walked into one of the school buildings a few hundred feet away. Ten minutes later, he returned and we were allowed to enter. No big deal, he said; the word *journalist* just made people nervous. I reminded him that although I was a journalist, I was also an academic, and because I was writing about the history of Cuban baseball, I preferred to use that term. Díaz subsequently introduced me to the coaches at the EIDE as a professor.

As we toured the school, I remembered having visited a facility identical in design, the Friedrich Engels school near Havana, almost twenty years earlier, on my first trip to Cuba in 1979. The Mártires de Barbados, which opened in 1977, had seen better days. It too was a victim of the "special period." No one seemed to care about upkeep, and I had to wonder whether the students really got the attention—or the food—they required. It seemed clear that the economic crisis affected even Cuba's elite sports programs. "The kids go home on weekends, and parents are encouraged to visit on Wednesdays. The province also provides a psychologist to help young players who are trying to be adults too soon, who are having trouble adapting, or whose home problems are affecting their school performance," writer Tom Miller noted about his visit to the Mártires de Barbados only a few weeks before I was there.[9]

Díaz took me down to the baseball diamonds, where the thirteen- to fourteen-year-old group was working out. These same fields had produced Orlando Hernández and Germán Mesa. In fact, 70 percent of the players on the two Havana teams, the Industriales and the Metropolitanos, hail from this school. It was 11:00 A.M., and the three-hour morning workout was just ending. After a break for lunch, the fifty young men attend classes during the afternoon. Evenings are split between studying and watching videos on baseball techniques. The fifteen- to sixteen-year-old group practices at 1:00 P.M. after attending classes in the morning.

"You have to have a great deal of patience to work with these young players," said Juan Bravo, one of the three coaches at the morning workout. Bravo, in his mid-thirties, had been a catcher with the Industriales. "They think they are men, but when they are under pressure, they often act like boys. In the *municipios*, each of these kids is the best in the town," explained Bravo. "All of the boys here think about being on *equipo Cuba*, although this is a bit far off for them. Most often, they dream about the next major tournament they will compete in."

"What are kids in the United States taught about baseball when they are thirteen?" asked Díaz on our return trip to Havana. "I know what we teach at that age. I know what they do in Japan." Díaz has been there five times as a coach for the International Baseball Association. "*Pero ellos no tienen la verdad. La verdad la tiene los Estados Unidos* [But they don't have the truth. The United States has the truth]. I want to know about baseball instruction for young people in the United States." He asked me to bring him some written material on the subject.[10]

Escuela Superior de Perfeccionamiento Atlético (Advanced School for Athletic Perfection)—ESPA

After age sixteen, those baseball players who show exceptional promise at the EIDEs are sent on to the Escuela Superior de Perfeccionamiento Atlético (Advanced School for Athletic Perfection)—ESPA, the next level of advancement for Cuban baseball prospects. There is one ESPA in each of Cuba's fourteen provinces, plus one for the city of Havana. At the ESPA, the best players from the province work on baseball four hours a day, six days a week, while they also attend school. The players who will represent Cuba in international competition—for example the Cuban junior team—are selected from the ESPA.[11]

By the time a Cuban prospect has completed the ESPA, or has arrived on a provincial team, he has received almost ten years of baseball instruction, has had a great deal of playing experience, and is in excellent physical condition.

Baseball Academies

There are fifteen baseball academies in Cuba, one in each province and another in Isla de la Juventud. The academy is where the players who have made it to the top of Cuba's baseball pyramid train. For example, the academy for the city of Havana is home to 185 players, including all of the players from the Industriales and the Metropolitanos, and their teams in the Serie de Desarrollo. All of the others who have advanced from the ESPA, and who play on teams in their home *municipios* between May and August, are also based at the academy.

The Cubans are searching not only for the best talent, but also for players who are willing to work hard and who fulfill some basic ideological criteria. At every step in the process, the Cubans work on the mental game, explaining the need to be patient, disciplined, and ready to adjust. "This is important, because sometimes the body develops and the mind stays behind," explained Valdés, "When you get the two together at a young age, this is exceptional."

"So this is how we prepare the kids," Valdés summed up. "They begin when they are four, and they continue to develop until they are ready to play in the Serie Nacional." The Cuban baseball league is currently structured into a sixteen-team league that plays a ninety-game schedule beginning in mid-October and ending in late March. Called the Serie Nacional, it has been the heart of Cuban baseball since 1961. This is the stage where Cuba's top players display their skills for the Cuban fans, while simultaneously trying to earn a spot on one of the teams that will represent Cuba abroad in international competitions.

The Serie Nacional, in its thirty-eighth season, has varied from four to eighteen teams and is now composed of one team from each of Cuba's fourteen provinces, one from the special municipality of Isla de la Juventud, and one additional team from the city of Havana. It is divided into four groups: Group A includes Pinar del Río, Isla de la Juventud, the Metropolitanos (Havana), and Matanzas; Group B consists of Havana Province, the Industriales (Havana), Sancti Spíritus, and Cienfuegos; Group C is concentrated in the center of the island and includes Villa Clara, Ciego de Ávila, Camagüey, and Las Tunas; and Group D in eastern Cuba has Holguín, Granma, Santiago de Cuba, and Guantánamo. In an effort to make baseball accessible to as many fans as possible, one game of each provincial team's home stand is played in a smaller town away from the provincial capital.

For most of the past thirty-eight years, the league played a shorter sixty-five-game schedule. At the conclusion, the best players were chosen to play on a reduced number of teams. This Serie Selectiva again served as a step in both showcasing the best baseball talent in Cuba and further reducing the pool available for international competitions. In the past, this second series has been composed of the top two teams of four divisions, or four teams representing the east, west, center, and metropolitan Havana area. In the mid-1990s, the Copa Revolucionaria replaced the Serie Selectiva but served the same function. In 1997, there was even a third series, pitting the best players from eastern and western Cuba in a two-week competition.

The current ninety-game schedule is followed by four best-of-five quarter final series, a best-of-seven semi-final series, and a best-of-seven championship series. The team that wins the Cuban championship does not automatically become *equipo Cuba*, but the winner of the Serie Nacional often represents Cuba in minor international competitions.

Serie de Desarrollo

Major league scouts often complain that while they can see Cuba's very best players at international competitions, very little is known about the other 350 players who participate in the Serie Nacional. And if little is known about these players, then an even more hidden source of baseball talent plays a regular season in almost complete obscurity. This source is the Serie de Desarrollo.

This league composed of younger prospects provides an opportunity for game experience for more than four hundred Cuban players. It has a parallel structure to the Serie Nacional, with sixteen teams. Like the players in the Serie Nacional, the vast majority of the players in the Serie de Desarrollo are products of an elite baseball production system, having passed through the EIDE and ESPA. Most of the players are still studying, working out in the afternoons, and playing games only on weekends, with a doubleheader on Saturday and a single game on Sunday.

Juan Castro, manager of the development team in Pinar del Río, was the catcher for *equipo Cuba* in 1987. Like many other retired players, Castro was brought into managing, and a few years ago he joined the large number of Cuban coaches who are contracted to teams overseas. Castro, age forty-four, has gone to Italy for the past six years. Not only does Castro learn more about baseball by managing Puerto Rican, Venezuelan, and Dominican players (as well as the best talent emerging in Italy), but he also brings home $5,000 or $6,000.

Castro was just completing a workout with his team at the Estadio Capitán San Luis in Pinar del Río when we spoke in 1998. He explained that the development team in Pinar del Río serves two different roles. First, it acts as taxi squad for the main team. He pointed out one of his players, Alay Soler, a third baseman, who had been brought up to replace the injured Omar Linares. The twenty-one-year-old Soler also throws ninety miles an hour and has a good slider. But this day Soler was returning to the development league team. Omar Linares was exercising and would play in that evening's game after missing almost a month of the season due to a knee injury.

The second, more important function of the parallel league is to give game experience to younger players. The development team is limited to players between the ages of seventeen and twenty-three. On each team there must be at least four players between the ages of seventeen and nineteen, and at least one of these youngsters must be in the game at all times.

While glancing at the roster of the Pinar del Río team, I noticed that most players had rather unusual names. "I have three relief pitchers with strange names, and I get them confused," explained Castro. "I just yell down to the bullpen, and say, 'Bring in the short guy.'" I never got the name of the short guy, but it was either Yariel, Ariel, or Raidel.

Equipo Cuba: Cuba's National Team

There is a great deal of confusion in the United States about what exactly the Cuban national team is. Some of this confusion stems from a lack of familiarity with the process of selecting the team in Cuba, and part comes from agents who are trying to inflate the credentials of a player who has defected.

The Cuban national team—or *equipo Cuba*—is basically equivalent to all-star teams of the U.S. major leagues, but because in Cuba there is only one league, there is also only one team. The twenty-four best Cuban players are selected each year to represent the country in international competitions. Prior to 1997, *equipo Cuba* had only twenty members; new international rules allowed for its expansion to twenty-two members in 1998, and to twenty-four in 1999. As the team is chosen, left-handed pitchers and good defensive players are often added to those with the highest batting averages and lowest ERAs. Because Cuba has so many international commitments, a second team called Cuba B is also selected. The combination of *equipo Cuba* and Cuba B is the rough equivalent of a major league team's forty-man roster.

The process for earning a position on Cuba's elite squad begins in earnest when a player is selected to compete on one of the sixteen teams in the Serie Nacional. At the end of the season, based on performance, the National Technical Commission of Cuban baseball chooses the top forty-five or fifty players to advance to the preselection training. Only those players who have participated in the season can be selected.

As part of this process, a detailed statistical analysis of the players invited to the preselection is compiled. In the stat book prepared in May of 1994, the selection criteria included performance based on a complicated system of analysis developed by the Cubans, "discipline and disposition of the players on and off the field,"[12] past international performances, and strength under pressure in game situations. The four-year Olympic cycle may also be taken into account when selecting a team for a given year. Thus, a player who has had a banner year might be kept off the team if he is considered too old for the Cuban Olympic team going to Sidney in 2000.

In 1993, I asked Valdés why a young player like Daniel Lazo, then nineteen, was included on the team brought to the United States. His candid reply was somewhat surprising: "Lazo plays all three outfield positions and first base, and he has great potential. We did not see him as a regular player on the team, because he is not ready. But we wanted him to see what it is like to prepare for *equipo Cuba*. He is from the countryside in Pinar del Río, and he needs to expand his horizons. He has spent most of his life in this isolated part of the country. Now when he goes home, he will think differently. He has been to Japan, Italy, the U.S. and he has played against those teams. This will help him later on. You can't do this with a young player from the capital, because he begins to think he is entitled to be there, and he won't train as hard."

San José de las Lajas: Forming Team Cuba

For all major sports in which Cuba competes internationally, there is a national training center. For much of the 1990s, the one for baseball was located at San José de las Lajas sports complex in Havana province, about twenty miles from Havana. Here, at what some Cuban journalists refer to as the "Millington of Cuba" (Millington, Tennessee, used to be the training site of USA Baseball before 1997), the players, now known as *preselección nacional*—or the core group of the team, which will represent Cuba in the year's international competition—embarks on a rigorous schedule of training. Over a period of a month, cuts are made until the team is narrowed to twenty-five players.

In the late 1990s, Cuban baseball officials began to rotate the training center among various sites, including San José de las Lajas, Morón in Ciego de Ávila province, and the Estadio Latinoamericano in Havana. There are also plans to utilize facilities in Las Tunas province and at Güines in Havana province.

After a few weeks of training, *equipo Cuba* travels to Pastejé, the training facility of the Mexico City Tigers of the Mexican League, about two hours west of Mexico City and over 9,000 feet above sea level. Here the Cubans engage in what they term *entrenamiento de altura* (altitude training). The Cuban technical staff sees this stamina building training, which has taken place annually for the past thirteen years, as one of the keys to the success of *equipo Cuba* later in the summer.

Since 1986, the Cuban team has made at least one trip each year to Pastejé. Valdés had read widely, especially in literature from the Soviet Union and East Germany, about the effects of training athletes at higher altitudes. While distance runners routinely engage in this type of training, it had never been used in baseball. Valdés decided to give it a try, and many in the Cuban sports establishment thought he had lost his mind. "The first time we did altitude training, it was a disaster. But we had to learn from our experience," explained Valdés. When Valdés suggested the team go the following year, Cuban sports officials told him, "Fine, if it doesn't work, it's your problem, and if it is successful, you can take the credit."

The Cuban players, who normally train at sea level and who will play most of their games at the same altitude, gradually adjust to working out in the thin air at Pastejé. The first day they begin by simply walking, working slowly until by the twelfth day they carry out the same routines they do in Cuba. The team trains for about twenty-five days. "Thirty days after the return to sea level, the players achieve the maximum benefits of the altitude training, and after fifty-five days, the effectiveness is lost," explained Valdés. With a window of only twenty-five days, Cuban officials have to be careful in scheduling the time in Pastejé in relation to the year's major international tournaments.

Skeptical of the value of what I thought might be just another excess of Eastern European training, I asked Valdés what tangible result he could show me. "With the improvement in bat speed," Valdés proudly explained, "on average, the Cuban players can see the ball for seven more feet—on a ninety-mile-an-hour pitch—before swinging. The batter can select a better pitch to hit." Other Cuban baseball officials insist that the altitude training improves a player's speed on the base paths as well as his resistance.

After returning from altitude training, the elite Cuban squad is trimmed to twenty-four players and usually plays a few exhibition series before competing in the year's premier international competition: the Olympics, the Pan American Games, or the Intercontinental Cup. Between 1986 and 1996, the tune-up games included a four-game series with Team USA and usually a few games against Japan's international amateur selection. In 1997, the Cubans canceled their U.S. tour at the last minute, and in 1998 and 1999 they turned down invitations to play at the new USA training site in Tucson, Arizona.

For ten years, between 1987 and 1997, the Cubans did not lose a single game in official international competitions, a winning streak of 150 games [their last loss was to Team USA at the Pan American Games in Indianapolis in 1987]. The Cuban team, with an average age of over twenty-nine, and with a core of players who had been together for most of those ten years, simply won at will.

There were no smiles on the faces of the Cuban players and coaches as they accepted the award for second place in the Intercontinental Cup in Barcelona in 1997. With its entire baseball system geared to winning international tournaments, Cuba is not accustomed to losing.

"I must confess that I do not know how to write about defeat," lamented *Granma*'s Sigfredo Barros in the lead to his story about Cuba's 11–2 loss to Japan in the championship game. Someone had to be blamed for the embarrassing defeat. Miguel Valdés was fired, along with *equipo Cuba* manager Jorge Fuentes. Not only did Cuba's baseball establishment have to explain to Fidel why they lost, but they also had to answer to Cuba's baseball fans, who are the world's most knowledgeable and enthusiastic.

"When I wrote about baseball in Cuba, I would receive letters from fans saying I made an error in a particular article," explained Dihigo. "That's why it is so difficult to be the manager of *equipo Cuba*, because there are ten million managers." The "ten million managers," a reference to the total population of Cuba (now numbering almost twelve million) is commonly used on the island to describe the willingness of the majority of the Cuban population to give its opinion on all aspects of baseball, from the selection of the national team to a pitch selection in the previous evening's game. How, I wondered, did these fans receive the detailed information about baseball that they always seemed to have at their fingertips?

emesio Guilló, the man who first brought baseball to Cuba in 1864, throwing out the rst ball at a veteran's game in Havana in 1922. Author's collection.

Awards ceremony for Cuba's top athletes. Havana, January 1997. Photo: Tim Wendel.

Left to right: Orestes Kindelán (Cuba's all-time home run leader), Miguel Valdés, and Omar Linares at the awards ceremony for Cuba's gold medal winners from the 1996 Olympics. Havana, January 1997. Photo: Tim Wendel.

Omar Linares in 1992 in Holguín before a game against the Olympic team.
Photo: Luis Hernández Iglesias. Author's collection.

Omar "El Niño" Linares in 1985, when he was eighteen years old. Author's collection.

Peña Deportiva Parque Central in front of the José Martí statue. *Left to right:* Antonio Hernández (who died in 1998), Orestes Llorente, Asdrubal Baró, an unidentified Peña member, Enrique Marrero, the author, Marcelo Sánchez, an unidentified gentleman, and Peter Bjarkman. The photo was taken by Mark Rucker, another Peña member. Parque Central, Havana, December 1997. Photo: Mark Rucker, Transcendental Graphics.

The author (*left*) with Marcelo Sánchez. Parque Central,
Havana, January 1997. Photo: Tim Wendel.

Esquina caliente. Parque Central, Havana, January 1997. Photo: Tim Wendel.

Asdrubal Baró at Estadio Latinoamericano, March 1998. Baró played in the
U.S. minor leagues and in the Cuban professional leagues in the 1940s and 1950s.
Photo: Greg Grieco.

Liván Hernández, 1998. In July 1999, Hernández was traded to the San Francisco Giants. Photo: Denis Bancroft. Courtesy of the Florida Marlins.

PLAYER _____ Hernandez _____ Orlando _____ OFP # __48__
_____ last _____ first _____ middle

Date of Birth ___101165___ Ht. _6-1_ Wt. _190_ Bats _R_ Throws _R_ Pos. _RHP_

School/Team ___Cuban National Team___ City ___Havana___ State _Cuba_

School Type _____ (HS, JC, 4YR) Stat _____ (5YR, DO, NS) Grad Date _____ Class _____

Comments _____

Curr Add _____ Perm Add _____
_____ (if different)

City/St ___Pinar del Rio, Cuba___ City/St _____

Zip _____ Telephone _____ Zip _____ Telephone _____

Scout ▓▓▓▓▓▓ Report Type _FOL_ (FOL, FCH) Report Date _081590_

Try out camp location _____ City _____ State _____

Summer Club ___Cuban National Team___ City ___Havana___ State _Cuba_

School next year _____ City _____ State _____

Games _1_ Inn. _1_ Filmed _____ Comments _____

RATING KEY	NON-PITCHERS	Pres.	Fut.	PITCHERS	Pres.	Fut.	USE WORD DESCRIPTION	
8—Outstanding	Hitting Ability	★		Fast Ball	★ 5	5	Habits	Good
7—Very Good	Power	★		F.B. Movement	6	6	Dedication	Good
6—Above Average	Running Speed	★		Curve	★ 4	5	Agility	Good
5—Average	Base Running			Control	4	5	Aptitude	Good
4—Below Average	Arm Strength	★		Change of Pace	0	0	Phys Maturity	Good
3—Well Below Average	Arm Accuracy			Slider	★ 0	0	Emot. Maturity	Good
2—Poor	Fielding	★		Other	★ 0	0		
Use One Grade	Range			Poise	4	5	Date eligible	
Grade On Major	Baseball Instinct			Baseball Instinct	5	5		
League Standards	Aggressiveness			Aggressiveness	5	5		
Not Amateur	Pull ___ Str Away ___ Opp Field ___			Arm Action Good Delivery Good				

Physical Description

Tall, strong pitchers build. Long arms and legs.

Gls/Contacts _NK_ Injs/Medical Update

No known injuries.

Abilities

3/4 del. Live FB has sinking, boring action to
RHH. CB just slurve, lacks tight rot and break.
FB 85-87

Weaknesses

Needs to improve CB and develop some type change.

Summation

Only saw one inning but showed live arm and
enough FB to warrant report.

Scouting report on Orlando Hernández.

Germán Mesa, October 1998. Photo: Ricardo López.

Germán Mesa (*far left*) returning to the field after an almost two-year suspension and being greeted by opposing players, October 18, 1998. Photo: Ricardo López.

Estadio Latinoamericano, Havana, 1991. Photo: Ricardo López.

Ernesto "Chico" Morilla holding a statue of Stan Musial. Estadio
Latinoamericano, March 1998. Musial gave Morilla the statue
in 1949 after Morilla struck him out in an exhibition game in
Houston. Photo: Greg Grieco.

Houston Astros hitting instructor Deacon Jones with a Cuban catcher at the Astros' clinic at Estadio Latinoamericano, 1977. Photo courtesy of Tal Smith.

ɔuston Astro Bob Watson at a clinic in Estadio Latinoamericano in 1977. Other Astros in ᵉ photo (*left to right*) are hitting instructor Deacon Jones (4), manager Bill Virdon, and .os Cabel (22). Two of the Cuban players are Antonio Muñoz (5) and Alfonso Urquiola, ɔ managed the Cuban team that faced the Baltimore Orioles in 1999. Photo courtesy of . Smith.

Houston Astros pitching coach Mel Wright with Cuban pitchers in Estadio Latinoamericano, 1977. Photo courtesy of Tal Smith.

José Ibar baseball card. Photo: Norman García. Courtesy of Cubadeportes, S.A. and García Photo Ltd.

Germán Mesa baseball card. Photo: Norman García. Courtesy of Cubadeportes, S.A. and García Photo Ltd.

Javier Méndez baseball card. Photo: Norman García. Courtesy of Cubadeportes, S.A. and García Photo Ltd.

Omar Linares baseball card. Photo: Norman García. Courtesy of Cubadeportes, S.A. and García Photo Ltd.

LANZADOR/PITCHER
PEDRO LUIS LAZO

Pedro Luis Lazo baseball card. Photo:
Norman García. Courtesy of Cubadeportes, S.A. and García Photo Ltd.

4 ☆ How Ten Million Managers Learn about Baseball

In November 1958, less than two months before he marched into Havana, Fidel Castro ventured out of the Sierra Maestra at the head of a small column of rebels. In the small town of Guisa, Fidel's men stocked up on provisions and asked residents about government troop movements. The *comandante* himself, on his first trip out of the mountains in almost three years, chose another way to reach the hearts and minds of the country folk. Sitting on a box in a grocery store, he talked baseball. "He had hoped to learn why Milwaukee's Carleton Willey, who had received the 'rookie of the year' award of the *Sporting News*, pitched only one inning in the World Series, while the veteran Warren Spahn started three games," writes Castro biographer Robert Quirk. "With Willey on the mound in the seventh and deciding game, he [Castro] said, the Braves might have defeated the Yankees."[1]

Fast-forward to the 1997 World Series. A Cuban is pitching for one of the competing teams. His countrymen from Havana to Santiago are following the games as closely as they can. But even though the one-time guerrilla with a passion for baseball has been running the country for over forty years, his countrymen get no help from their own media. Cuban newspapers, radio, and TV stations, all government-owned, treat the Series, and the rest of major league ball, as if it doesn't exist. While Fidel may still appreciate the game itself, his government treats professional ball as an arm of the U.S. empire. Even when a

Cuban is a key player in the Series? Especially when a Cuban is a key player. World Series MVP Liván Hernández had defected from Cuba.

The defectors may represent everything that the Cuban government detests about the magnetic attractions of the United States, but Cubans who have no intention of heading for Miami would love to have better access to broadcasts, statistics, and other player information. Over the years, they've built what amounts to their own baseball information network, unorganized but reaching every corner of the country. I joined it simply by mailing newspaper and magazine clippings to my friends on the island and by bringing baseball publications with me on my trips to Cuba. Relatives visiting loved ones on the island do the same. The information then gets spread by hand or through the national grapevine known as *radio bemba*—street gossip.

This may be a testament to Cuban ingenuity and baseball fervor, but it also seems pointless. If Cubans manage to follow professional ball without any help from their media, and if Cuban journalists would love to cover it, why keep up the information embargo? The question sounds reasonable, but only to someone who doesn't factor in forty years of U.S.-Cuba hostility. The official boycott of the major leagues makes as much sense as anything else growing out of that singularly bizarre bilateral relationship.

What surprised me though, as I immersed myself in the island's baseball culture, was that keeping up with Cuban baseball isn't always easy, either. Cuban fans wistfully recall a golden age in the 1960s and 1970s when the government published a volume of stats after each Serie Nacional. Recently, conditions have begun to improve somewhat, although *Granma*, the country's dominant newspaper and the official organ of the Cuban Communist Party, now publishes little about the country's number one sport. Printed five days a week, with a circulation of 400,000, *Granma* not only doesn't carry box scores from Cuban games, but it prints few statistics at all, except for occasional lists of the top five batters or pitchers. *Juventud Rebelde*, which returned to publishing daily in 1999, has a few baseball stories each week, and the monthly magazine *Bohemia* also covers the national sport.

The reason for this lack of coverage, as I learned from my Cuban friends, is also political. In a country that is famously and tragically dependent on one crop—sugar cane—Fidel didn't want Cuba to remain a two-sport country, with only baseball and boxing dominating. Adopting the East German strategy of building international prestige by winning Olympic medals, Cuba aims to develop world-class athletes in a variety of sports. So when it comes to baseball, the media keep the volume down—not off, but not loud either. Cuba isn't a soccer country, but Cuban TV broadcast live every game of the 1998 World Cup. *Tododeporte*, the major Sunday TV sports show, does show some Cuban baseball games—along with badminton, boxing, gymnastics, and volleyball. The show even carries the occasional National Basketball Association (NBA) game. Cuban government officials insist that they have nothing to do with professional sports, which they call a capitalist perversion of athletics. So how do NBA games get on the tube? Basketball, one young fan explained to me, isn't part of the Cuban heritage, so the island's budding hoopsters are unlikely to flee Cuba to try to play for the Chicago Bulls. But, he said, "The government believes that talking about major league baseball might stimulate defections."

In one sense, neither the information ban on professional baseball nor the low-key approach to Cuban ball matters much. This is still a country where every family has at least one baseball fanatic, and where the game is so embedded in the culture that, just as in the United States, its expressions are part of everyday speech. When a conversation is veering into sensitive territory, someone is likely to say, *"discutamos de pelota"* (let's talk baseball). As Fidel undoubtedly realized when he decided to downplay baseball, it doesn't need a lot of official support to flourish.

The statue of Cuban patriot José Martí looms over Havana's Parque Central. Fortunately, so do dozens of palm trees that provide shelter from Cuba's blazing sun for a constant parade of strollers—and hustlers selling cigars, old baseball cards, and just about anything that can be bought, sold, or traded. But the passersby and street corner merchants are only a sideshow in the block-long park, which adjoins a boulevard leading to the fabled waterfront avenue, the Malecón. The main attraction is provided by the ten or so groups of a half-dozen men each (I've never seen a woman) who gather each day on the south side of the park to trade baseball information, discuss strategy and, above all, to argue so loudly and passionately that a non–Spanish speaker might think he'd stumbled on the birthplace of the next Cuban revolution. Cubans call anywhere that people gather to talk baseball the *esquina caliente* (hot corner), but the park is the hottest corner of all.[2]

"*Chico*, why are you talking about a subject you know nothing about?" yelled one young guy to another with whom he was nose-to-nose, in the classic posture of umpire and player. The other fellow didn't have a comeback, effectively bringing that debate to an end. The debate's protagonists had gotten so loud and so aggressive that, for onlookers, the subject matter got lost somewhere along the way.

"Everybody in Cuba has an opinion about baseball and wants to be a manager," says Lázaro Luis González, a good friend and researcher at the University of Havana who has been a baseball devotee since he was a member of the Cuban equivalent of Little League. He was the kind of kid who suffered even when his team won if he didn't consider his playing to be worthy.

Lázaro Luis approaches the game like the scholar he is. "Not all Cubans have a profound analysis of baseball," he said as we walked through the park. "Fans argue about superficial things like who is a better player, and they shout at each other, rather than sitting down and discussing baseball in an analytical way. As the saying goes, Cuba could have ten million managers—but a lot of them would be bad."

Maybe so, but in a country where people don't feel free to talk openly about political or social issues, the *esquina caliente* provides the liveliest public debate in the country. When I first visited the park in 1992, one group was talking about Cuban baseball of the 1950s, another was dissecting Cuba's national team, and yet another was focusing on the careers of U.S. players from the 1940s and 1950s. Entranced, I went from circle to circle, moving on when boredom or curiosity about the next group set in. Whether their opinions were sound or off base, clearly these were all men whose lives centered on the game. And a lot of the talkers seemed to be well-accustomed to talking to each other.

A friend had given me the name of a fan to look for. I approached one group, introduced myself as a baseball writer from the United States, and asked for Marcelo Sánchez. After looking me up and down and asking questions that resonated with suspicion, one of the debaters motioned for me to follow. We walked about a block through the center of Old Havana. Then my guide stopped and, looking toward the top of an aged apartment building, boomed out "Marcelo!" It was the Cuban version of a house-phone call. Moments later, a woman appeared at a fourth-floor window. "*Está bañando* [He's taking a bath]," she yelled. So much for private life in Havana's densely populated neighborhoods.

Marcelo soon appeared on the street. A short, thin man with a full head of white hair, Sánchez is a retired linotypist (a job that in the United States has disappeared in the computer age) living on a pension of a couple of hundred pesos a month—the equivalent of about $10 U.S. He is especially expert on the subject of Cubans who have played professional ball in the United States. I told him that Tony Menéndez had been called up by Cincinnati. "He's number 128," Sánchez shot back.

Marcelo became a fast friend. In between my trips to the island, we stayed in touch by mail or by letters hand delivered by friends and acquaintances traveling to and from Cuba.[3] This contact allowed me to keep him supplied with articles about how Cuban players were doing in the United States. When I was in Cuba, Marcelo became one of my guides through the baseball universe, of which the park debates are only a small part. He also showed me that the park scene isn't as unorganized as it seems at first. For one thing, the park is the headquarters of an officially registered baseball fan organization, the Peña Deportiva Parque Central, *peña* being Spanish for a gathering of connoisseurs. It has 140 dues-paying members, plus 12 honorary ones, myself included, who pay their dues in dollars. It is Cuba's answer to the Society for American Baseball Research.

Members draw a line between their formal gatherings and the unstructured discussions in the park, in which they're all fervent participants. But, this being Cuba, even the "formal" sessions might strike a *yanqui* as only somewhat less passionate than, say, the scene in the bleachers during the ninth inning of a hot game. During one meeting at the park in 1997, at which Tim Wendel of *Baseball Weekly* and I were given the honor of addressing, I got a hint of what it must be like to make a good play in a Cuban stadium when a member asked why so many Dominicans are playing in the United States. A roar of approval went up when I responded, "They got a chance to play when the Cuban players quit going."

Even among these hyperinvolved, often argumentative fans, certain topics require delicate handling. "What do you think of professionals in the Olympics?" one member asked. Tim replied, "Let the best play against the best." His comment was greeted with silence. Or perhaps a later question was a form of response: "Do you believe the Cuban national team is really challenged by the level of competition it plays?" Tim and I both said no. Heads nodded all around.

Every now and then, the Peña gets to move its serious meetings indoors, away from the hurly-burly of the street. One day in December 1997, I dropped by the park to find Marcelo and ended up again heading for his apartment, without a guide this time. I couldn't remember the number of his building, but I found it eventually with the help of a clerk in a nearby store. The building used to house the Hotel Monserrat and like many, if not most, of the apartment buildings where ordinary citizens live, it doesn't seem to have been maintained—not even with a coat of paint—since the late 1950s. Up a stairwell lit by only one bulb, I made my way to Marcelo's tiny, sparsely furnished apartment, which he and his wife, Lucila, share with their dog, Malú, and with shelves and cabinets packed with old baseball cards and volumes of baseball statistics, some that have reached him from the United States and some that he has compiled himself.

He thanked me for the latest copy of *Baseball Weekly* and then invited me and a couple of other U.S. writers visiting Havana that week to give an *informe*—the word means a formal report—to the Peña. Marcelo had even reserved a room, he said, at El Chocolate. When I heard that, I thought he was talking about one of the new cafés that have opened in the past five years in Old Havana for the benefit of tourists, mostly Europeans and Canadians, flocking to Cuba. I wondered how the Peña could afford such a luxury because these places charge in dollars. It soon became clear he was talking about a gymnasium named for Kid Chocolate, a famous Cuban boxer of the 1930s. It was built for the 1991 Pan American Games in front of the old capitol building on a site where some dilapidated residential buildings had been demolished. It is now used for basketball, volleyball, boxing, and karate lessons for kids and for adult exercise classes. The gym's managers try to meet the Peña's need for a meeting room. So far, the organization hasn't been able to get the permanent quarters they'd like, with storage space for their records and a TV and VCR to watch baseball videos.

About ten members, age fifty and over, showed up. Among them was Asdrubal Baró, who had played in 1956 for my hometown team, the Double A Houston Buffs. We had planned on meeting for an hour, ended up talking for three, and could have stayed all night. While members stay true to their tradition of letting everyone speak his mind, they can't help but fall into the patterns of a country where people often make a point of talking about their sensitive subjects without naming names. "Baseball has a business factor," Aurelio Alonzo, who looks like a slightly younger version of Montreal Expos manager Felipe Alou, began. "I'm talking about the team that won the World Series," he said, refraining from naming the Florida Marlins, who attracted so much Cuban interest because they play in Miami and because Liván Hernández joined them fresh from Cuba.

"We don't really understand how it works as a business," Alonzo continued. "And that is what we are interested in. Maybe you gentlemen can help us." With that, we got into a lively discussion that touched on the Marlins unloading their high-salaried players, the possibility of franchises moving, new stadiums, and the distinction between big-market and small-market teams. I'm used to having to prod discussions along in the classes I teach at the University of Texas. Here, the talk just flowed without a lull, and many questions remained when we called a halt. It amounted to a perfect graduate seminar.

Unlike the *esquina caliente* debates, the formal discussion takes place without posturing or shouting. Members don't interrupt each other, but mostly preface their comments with respectful references to the previous speaker—"I'm in agreement with the *compañero*," or "He may have a point, but I would like to disagree." I asked about the age of Tampa Bay pitcher Rolando Arrojo, who defected in 1996, claiming he was twenty-eight. There was some discussion of whether he was thirty-two or thirty-three, but all agreed that there was no way he was under thirty. At the same time, participants pointed out that shaving a few years off one's age is a tradition that predates defections. "When I signed with the Dodgers in 1951, Al Campanis told me to take off three years," says Baró. "When I was signed by the St. Louis Cardinals in 1956, I was twenty-nine; the scout told me to put down twenty-five."

The Peña members welcomed foreigners, at least this one, saying things that ordinary Cubans don't seem to feel comfortable saying out loud. I suggested that, with professionals now allowed to participate in the Olympics, Cubans ought to have a chance to play in the U.S. major leagues and then come home for winter ball in Cuba. That way, neither players nor fans would suffer the breaking of the bond that's now the inevitable consequence of a player's going pro. In addition, the players would sharpen their skills by playing at a higher competitive level. The bottom line would be a much-improved Olympic team from Cuba. Peña members, exaggerating the extent of my influence, urged me to talk up the plan. "You know a lot of people in the media here," said one. "Why don't you tell them, so more people here in Cuba can know about it?" In fact, I did tell my Cuban journalist friends, but I'm not holding my breath waiting for them to get clearance to write about the idea.

A sore point with the Peña was what they called the misrepresentation of the scene at the Parque Central when the 1997 World Series was played. What they meant was that those following the games in the park had been labeled as "la Peña." This was a serious issue for men who didn't want to get lumped in with others who criticized the government in the foreign press. "You probably heard about the crowds in the park supporting the Marlins and especially Liván Hernández," Alonzo said. "When some foreign reporters came, several people talked with them and claimed to be from the Peña, but they didn't belong to our group. We heard about this and we went to the Partido [Communist Party], to the *municipio*, and to INDER, and we showed them our membership list and explained that none of the people who made the comments to the press were our members."

Of course, the park was an obvious place for foreign reporters to visit during the Series. *El Nuevo Herald*, the Spanish-language daily published by the *Miami Herald*, even reported that the police asked a crowd of about 150 people listening to the series on five transistor radios in the park to move to another location so that foreign guests at the Hotel Inglaterra, which faces the park, wouldn't be disturbed. The paper called the group "la Peña." In fact, Alonzo says, most of the Peña members caught the games at home. "Many of us listened to the games on the radio, and some even paid 20 pesos to watch the game on TV in houses that had a special antenna." He meant an illegal antenna that picks up transmissions to satellite dishes parked on the roofs of tourist hotels.[4]

Most of the Peña members heard the games on WCMQ, a Miami Spanish-language station, one of the Florida stations that can be heard in Cuba.[5] While they enjoyed most of the commentary by announcers Felo Ramírez and Manolo Alvarez, members took exception to remarks by the two to the effect that no one in Cuba was talking about Fidel Castro, but instead about Liván Hernández. "They tried to link our interest in Liván to a protest against the government," Alonzo said. "And that was just not so."

Alonzo said that a BBC reporter had tried to interview him about Hernández. "She asked me about *el caso de Liván Hernández*. I told her, 'I don't know *el caso de Liván Hernández*; I know Liván Hernández.'" He added, "We had seen him pitch here in Cuba and knew how talented he was. He is good because of his natural ability and because he came from a baseball program here in Cuba that developed his skills." Clearly, the fans had some reservations about Liván, which they attributed to the manner in which he defected, taking off during a team trip to Mexico. "We do not question Liván's decision to leave," Alonzo said. "That is his personal choice. We only question the method by which he chose to leave: while representing his country abroad."

By the next time I delivered an *informe*, in early 1998, Liván's brother Orlando had defected, taking off from Cuba by boat. No one had a bad word to say about him. There was a feeling hanging in the air, but never spelled out, that the Cuban government had left him no choice but to take off—more because the sports bureaucracy had blocked his athletic career after Liván's defection than because of the contrast between his hard-scrabble existence on the island and a multimillion-dollar career in the majors.

Any Cuban, of course, understands why someone reaches the point where he or she can't take the privations of life on the island. The first time I met Marcelo, I asked as we walked if there was anything he needed. "Milton, I don't like to ask for anything, but I could use a good cigar," he said. The best ones are reserved for the tourist trade, and we headed for a "dollar store" just behind the Floridita, which was one of Ernest Hemingway's haunts. We entered the dollar store, and Marcelo selected the smallest available cigar. I suggested he take a couple of the jumbo, nine-inch *tabacos*, and he did. They sell for $8, nearly as much as Marcelo's monthly stipend. But I had forgotten something, and obviously I still didn't understand how tight things were for ordinary Cubans. As we walked out of the store, Marcelo turned to me saying, "Milton, I don't have any matches." On my most recent visit to his apartment, I noticed that the front door to his building is now locked. Life is getting very tough indeed when people as hard up as Marcelo and his neighbors have to take defensive measures.

For some of Marcelo's fellow members, lifetimes of hard work also include decades of front-line combat. One day, Antonio Hernández, a rail-thin, bespectacled Peña member in his mid-sixties, told me at some length about his military history, starting with the revolution that brought Fidel to power in 1959, continuing with counterinsurgency warfare against guerrillas in the Escambray mountains in the 1960s, and followed by service with Cuban forces in the 1970s during the brutal campaigns in Angola and Ethiopia. He told me how he had watched one of his comrades die, figuring that he himself would be next, when his unit was trapped in a canyon in Ethiopia by Somali troops. Only a last-minute breakthrough by Cuban and Soviet forces saved Antonio and his men.

Despite the hard times they endure, Antonio and his fellow fans discussed the details of Orlando Hernández's contract with the New York Yankees without any signs of jealousy. And they knew more than I did. Hernández had been signed just as I got to Cuba. Cut off from my normal sources of information, I pled ignorance during one street-corner conversation with a fan who wanted to know the details of the contract. Then Marcelo showed up. "It was $6.6 million for four years," he said, which turned out to be precisely the case.

Television may be taking over the world, but Cuba is still radio territory. In a country where frequent electricity blackouts ruin many a night of TV-watching, the battery-powered radio is a more dependable companion. When the Cuban national baseball team plays in an important international competition, nearly every radio in Cuba seems to be tuned to the game, and a passerby can follow the action just by walking down the street as the entire island transforms itself into one big receiving station. Among a people who depend on radio in ways that recall pre-TV America, baseball fans are the most devoted listeners of all. "In the early 1980s, people listened to major league games on short-wave and passed the scores around as if they were in a secret society," journalist Gilberto Dihigo recalled.

One night in 1997, I dropped by the studios of Radio Rebelde to sit in on the country's most influential sports show, *Deportivamente*. The five-night-a-week, 8:30–10:30 P.M. show owes its position not only to its on-air personalities but also to the reach of the station's signal. In addition to the entire island, it reaches into Central and South America, as well as into the southern United States.[6] During the Atlanta Olympic Games in 1996, the station broadcast eighteen hours a day. Pedro Cruz González, who produces *Deportivamente*, said, "We even received thank-you calls from people in Miami"—not something Cuban radio shows are generally accustomed to.

He talked to me as we sat in the control room, in studios that once served as the official radio station of Fulgencio Batista, the dictator whom the rebels overthrew in 1959. A lot of the equipment Batista's engineers left behind is still running, in the same mysterious way as the

1950s Chevies, Fords, and Plymouths that every American visiting Cuba notices immediately as the cars rumble down the streets.

Deportivamente aims to cover all sports topics, but there is no question which sport dominates. On the night I visited, the show began with a discussion of games set for the next day, with one of the three hosts, Ramón Rivera, reminding fans that the Industriales, Havana's favorite team, would play Villa Clara in the Estadio Latinoamericano in the capital. A report followed from the eastern province of Holguín, where fans complained that local government big shots had reserved the best seats for themselves at a recent game. That sort of criticism is standard for Cuban radio, which serves as a sounding board for complaints against the government or functionaries that never find their way into print.

Then the phone started ringing. One caller asking about home run leaders in Cuba sent Arnelio Alvarez, the show's official statistician, to his record books. Another asked about an injury to the extremely popular third baseman for the Industriales, Lázaro Vargas—prompting the producer to call Vargas at home to ask how he was doing (he wasn't home).

The main topic that callers raised was retirement. Once over-thirty Cuban players retire, they are contracted through Cubadeportes to play overseas [this is examined in detail in Chapter 5]. But a retired player can't come back to Cuba to play ball. "Many of our callers believe too much attention is given to the selection of *equipo Cuba*," says producer Cruz González. "They say letting players retire is good for Cuba, but bad for baseball in Cuba. How do you explain the policy to a fan whose team lost the first three batters in its lineup?"

Two topics don't come up on this, or any other, Cuban radio show: players who have defected and U.S. major league ball. Clearly, the first is extremely sensitive, politically speaking. The status of the second is fuzzier. At one time, fans say, Cruz González began reporting big league scores and commenting on games. That makes sense; in the late 1960s, he was one of the first radio deejays who dared to play the Beatles on air. Up to that point, they and all other "decadent" rock musicians were nonpersons on Cuban airwaves. Musical standards loosened up years ago, but Cruz González has dropped his small-scale coverage of the majors.

In conversation, Cruz González makes clear that, like every Cuban baseball fan, he follows major league activities as closely as he can. "I'm really sad that the Dodgers are being sold," he said, only days after the fact. "I interviewed Peter O'Malley a few years ago, and I want to see a game in Dodger Stadium before he sells the team."

Because of the constraints on public speech, it wasn't unusual for me to learn as much from talking to Cruz González as from listening to the show he produces. Likewise for my encounters with baseball writers. That aside, both in print and conversation, Cuban sportswriters maintain a high level of dispassionate professionalism, without the vulgarity and name-calling in which some of their U.S. counterparts often engage. The *Granma* baseball writer Sigfredo Barros, a fifty-two-year-old ringer for Gabriel García Márquez, the Nobel Prize–winning novelist from Colombia (and close friend of Fidel's), knows as much about Cuban baseball as anyone in the country. A swimmer and polo player in his youth, Barros's first and most enduring love is baseball. He didn't want to write about anything else. But midway through his twenty-seven-year career, he says, "I got assigned to cover all the sports that no one wanted to write about: fencing, cycling, and rowing." He's been back on the baseball beat since 1985. It's no secret to him that many readers would love to see major league news in the Cuban press. "But the official government policy is no professional sports."

Raúl Arce, 48, has been at *Juventud Rebelde* since he was twenty years old. I'd read his articles for years before finally meeting him in 1997. "One of the differences from the U.S. is that here, there are really no guides with ages and statistics. You have to talk to the players one by one. We don't have the organization to put together a statistical book," he told me as we watched the Industriales play Provincia Habana in March 1998.

Discussions with journalists who talked freely about matters they couldn't publish or say on the air—it made as much sense as anything else in a country where rules are inflexible one minute and nonexistent the next. Yet, notwithstanding the effects of an ideology born in Europe and muscled into power in Russia, Cuba remains a very Latin country, with a people as warm as the weather. Most important, bonds between individuals are often much more highly valued than rules and regulations.

In 1997, I was outside the Estadio Latinoamericano trying to explain to a guard who I was and why I should be let in. I wasn't getting very far. And then Héctor Rodríguez, Cuba's leading TV sports commentator, a star baseball analyst for more than 30 years, showed up. I had first run into Héctor in 1991 in Millington, Tennessee, of all places, where the USA-Cuba baseball tournament was being played. Hanging around the press box before the first game, I watched as Héctor and his radio colleague, a play-by-play announcer, discovered they had been assigned side-by-side seats, a setup that would have made their jobs all but impossible. The Cubans were having a hard time making their problem understood because they barely spoke English and hardly anyone on the U.S. side spoke Spanish. I stepped in as translator (as a native Texan, I even understood the Tennessee accents) and made sure that the Cubans got seats far enough apart that they didn't unwittingly interfere with each other's broadcasts.

Six years later, when Héctor appeared outside the stadium and greeted me, he let me stroll with him past the guard into the stadium. No guard was going to challenge someone of his stature; apart from his TV role, he's a member of Cuba's quasi-legislature and vice president of the Commission on Health, Sports, and the Environment. After the game, I told him I wanted to sit in on the following evening's broadcast of *Deportivamente*. When I showed up at the studio the next day, my name was on a list posted by the door—this in a country where reporters and academics without contacts can spend days or even weeks waiting for visits to be set up and interviews arranged, all the while being told that the rules don't allow any other way of proceeding.

The system's arbitrariness and rigidity is far tougher on Cubans, which is why they value personal contacts so highly. Navigating the red-tape maze without them would be unbearable, if not impossible. Cubans also know better than to try to decipher the logic of all official decisions. No one seems to know why Provincia Habana, the team from the rural fringe outside the city, rarely gets its games televised, but no one would waste the time to try to find out either. Or to try to find out why the government publishes a sports magazine but can't seem to get it distributed. "There is something called *Jit* [pronounced 'Hit'] which comes out each month and deals with baseball. I know it comes out, but I have never seen an issue," my friend Lázaro Luis González told me in 1997. To be sure, copies did start showing up on newsstands later that year—and the magazine includes detailed baseball statistics.

Then the government started up a news service carrying the most complete compilations of baseball statistics—and put it out of reach of most Cubans. *Marcas*, published by the official news agency, Prensa Latina, runs detailed stories on baseball players as well as a wealth of statistics. Yet it's only available on-line.[7] As far as most Cubans are concerned, that means it might as well be published on the moon. A people barely scraping by, worried about getting fresh batteries for their radios and keeping their refrigerator motors cranking, are not about to run out and buy computers. When Marcelo writes me, he does so on a 1918 typewriter. And his ribbons come from the States.

U.S. fans can do a lot of their game watching, baseball talking, and information trading over cold beers in a sports bar with TVs everywhere you look. Cuban fans do a lot of their talking on the street or in parks because there aren't any sports bars for ordinary Cubans. As for watching, a Cuban fan has a choice between the stadium and the living room.

When Fidel Castro wanted to speak to the nation during a crisis, he strode into the TV studio at a moment of extreme tension. It was August 1994. Cubans were stealing all kinds of vessels to try to reach the United States, and discontented youths had rioted in downtown Havana. The show on the air at the time was *Hoy Mismo*, a nightly news show hosted by Héctor Rodríguez. All of a sudden, Rodríguez was sharing his announcer's desk with the *comandante en jefe*. Every now and then, during his two-hour speech, Fidel would turn and, tapping on Rodríguez's arm, ask, "Isn't that right, Héctor?" Rodríguez would nod. Now the world's longest-tenured ruler, Castro didn't indulge in the baseball talk with which he used to reach out to people in his days up in the mountains. But it probably didn't make any difference because few Cubans saw him. *Hoy Mismo* has only a small share of the viewing audience, competing head on with the more popular telenovelas. The program remains on the air only because the *comandante en jefe* himself enjoys watching it.

5 ☆ "We Woke Up from the Dream Too Late": Crisis in Cuban Baseball

In Holguín, I experienced the sights and sounds of a jam-packed Cuban stadium. The gates of Estadio Calixto García opened at 10:00 A.M. for an 8:30 P.M. game between *equipo Cuba* and the team that would represent the United States in the 1992 Barcelona Olympics. It was the first time any Cuban national baseball team had played in Holguín, and by 10:30 A.M. the stadium—with a capacity of over thirty thousand—was half full. By 4:00 P.M. it was completely full, and government authorities estimated that there were fifty thousand people outside who could not get in.

Just before the game, a symphonic orchestra played the national anthems of both Cuba and the United States and then gave way to a salsa band. I, along with five other members of the foreign press, was seated directly behind home plate. While Cuban fans waited up to ten hours for the game, a group of Dutch and German tourists were ushered in just before the first pitch and seated in a section next to us. By game time the crowd was electric, and I was eager to see what an even larger crowd in Havana would be like.

The Estadio Latinoamericano in Havana is an impressive structure with a seating capacity of 55,000. But in 1997, like Cuban baseball itself, it was undergoing an overhaul. The dirt and grass on the playing field were new, but upon closer inspection, something was amiss. There were deep holes in the outfield grass, and the infield dirt stuck to shoes. Although the ten thousand sheet-metal panels on the roof that protected many of the fans from the rain and glaring sun had been replaced, for the last couple of seasons there had been few fans to protect. During the 1996–1997 season—the 36th Serie Nacional—only a couple of thousand fans attended a week-night game. Even during the playoffs between two of the best teams—Pinar del Río and the Industriales only five thousand or six thousand fans showed up. What was going on?

"I don't go to the games because it's too hard to get there," exclaimed the taxi driver taking me to the Estadio Latinoamericano. "Look around, we are driving on one of Havana's principal avenues on a Sunday afternoon, and you don't see a single bus." He was right. What accounted for the lack of transportation? The driver thought for a moment, searching for a way to explain to a foreigner the complexities that led to this very moment in the history of Cuba. "We woke up from the dream too late," he said. He went on to explain that Cuba was isolated from its nearest neighbor, the United States, and that the dream of socialism began to disintegrate when the Soviet Union fell apart. Cuba was indeed now cut off from the two foreign powers that had dominated its existence for the entire century.

There was no question that transportation was a problem. After a game on my first night in Havana in 1997, I sought a ride to my hotel, but only television announcer Héctor Rodríguez had a car. There were no other cars, taxis, or buses in sight. The stadium is well off the beaten path, and walking is the only sure way to get there. In the dozen times I attended games in 1997 and 1998, I walked to or from the stadium and my hotel room or apartment, using the opportunity to take in Havana's surreal beauty.

I recounted my experiences to Gilberto Dihigo, then in his third year away from Cuba, who was surprised to hear of the low game attendance. It was sad, I said, to go to this huge stadium for a game between Las Tunas and the Metropolitanos and see two, maybe three, thousand fans. "That's because Las Tunas ..." began Dihigo, and then stopped before saying that they were not a very good team, as many Cubans had already pointed out to me. "There is another problem: you can't forget the *espectáculo*. *Béisbol es un espectáculo* [Baseball is a show]. You can't put in a young kid who's just learning to play because you want to help develop a provincial team. The end result is that the team loses and people get bored and stop going to the games. Today there is an imbalance among the teams in the league."

The discussion turned to the attendance at the 5:00 P.M. Saturday doubleheader between two teams that had met in the finals the previous season, Villa Clara and the Industriales. "Then it was full, no?" inquired Dihigo, assuming there was a good crowd. No, I said. I explained that there were about eight thousand fans, and with the Industriales holding a big lead in the seventh inning in game one, almost everyone left, rushing to get home to see the second game or the Saturday night movie on television while there was still some type of public transportation available. I was among those fans leaving early so that I could make the forty-five minute walk back to my hotel before dark.[1] I told Dihigo how much I enjoyed walking the streets of Havana.

"And then you got to rest and have a good meal," said Dihigo. "But for the average Cuban to leave at the end the game and have no way to get home?" said Dihigo, shrugging his shoulders. "Baseball, which used to be a catharsis, has been converted into a penance, and the people don't want to punish themselves. They prefer to stay home."

In 1997, many in Havana were too busy trying to "resolve" their "necessities"—the two most often heard words in Cuba—to make baseball a priority. And there is no doubt that fans were upset with the quality of play and the defections and "early retirement" of some players. Four years earlier, Industriales fans would have seen Germán Mesa at short, with Rey Ordóñez as his backup, and Roberto Colina at first base. The pitching staff included Orlando Hernández, Liván Hernández, and Vladimir Núñez. All but Mesa have defected, and he was banned from Cuban baseball for life, allegedly for taking money from a U.S. baseball agent. That ban was lifted in 1998.

Although Cuba started charging admission for baseball games in 1994, it wasn't really a factor in the lower attendance figures because ticket prices remained very low: one peso (about five cents), or three pesos to sit behind home plate. But there has been an interesting twist connected to the admission charge.[2] Fans no longer return balls hit into the stands, at least not in Havana. In Holguín in 1992, I remember a home run hit into the outfield bleachers. Rather than the swarm of people fighting for the ball I was accustomed to seeing in the United States, I watched the crowd part so that no one would be hit, and then the fan who retrieved the ball tossed it back onto the field. Fans throwing back foul balls had developed into quite a tradition in Cuba. The ritual was both a political statement against the U.S. embargo and a necessity in a country short of resources.[3]

In 1997, I saw young boys selling baseballs in the stands of the Estadio Latinoamericano for one U.S. dollar. They were, of course, the foul balls and home run balls that were no longer being returned. The ideology that provided free admission had been swept away two seasons before, and now the tradition that accompanied it for more than thirty years had gone with it. "They quit throwing back the foul balls this year," lamented Marcelo Sánchez, as we watched a game in the Estadio Latinoamericano. "Nobody returns anything in Cuba today."

Equipo Cuba vs. Cuban Baseball

"There is a contradiction in Cuban baseball between *deporte* [sport] and *espectáculo* [show]," *Granma* beat writer Sigfredo Barros told me in 1997. "It is difficult to both win international tournaments and satisfy the fans at home."

Barros was referring to the challenge facing the Cuban sports program of both providing a quality baseball season between November and April and selecting a national team to represent Cuba in international competitions between June and August. At times, baseball officials have had to struggle to meet both goals. The *equipo Cuba* was expected to win gold medals at all costs, even if that meant providing a lesser quality product to very discerning Cuban fans at home.

"To me, the Serie Nacional is the most important sporting event in Cuba," explained Barros. "It is more important to Cuban fans than the international tournaments." But in the mid-1990s, the quality of Cuban baseball was declining both at home and abroad. Cuban officials began to be concerned after *equipo Cuba* lost four consecutive games to Team USA in 1995 in Millington, Tennessee.[4] While the Cubans remained undefeated in official international competitions until 1997, the national teams were clearly not the dominant squads of the previous decade. And the quality of play at home was sloppy, inconsistent, and unappealing to Cuban fans accustomed to watching high-quality baseball.

The problems Cuban baseball faced in 1997 were multifaceted and ranged from the fall of communist governments in Eastern Europe to a lack of adequate pitching instruction. Interestingly, a great deal of the complaining about the poor state of baseball came from inside Cuba;

adverse comments appeared in the government-controlled press, and criticism was the main topic of radio talk shows as well as the daily fare of the *esquina caliente.*

"At this time, Cuban baseball has the same chemical properties as water: colorless, odorless, and flat," remarked sportswriter Enrique Capetillo in a commentary on Radio Rebelde.[5] "The Cubans play with reluctance and without the passion they used to have. You can see it in the way they run the bases and the way they swing at any pitch. This sets a bad example for kids who watch the games . . . and see the way their idols trot instead of run. The result is that people are not going to the games," noted Capetillo. "*Cada vez hay menos espectáculos* [Each time there is less of a show]."

At the *esquina caliente* and in the Peña, fans complained about the selection process of *equipo Cuba* and the quality of play in the Serie Nacional. They were openly critical of manager Jorge Fuentes and technical director Miguel Valdés. The year before there were even banners displayed at the Estadio Latinoamericano lamenting the state of baseball. In a country where most decisions are decreed with no questions asked, there was a true groundswell of demand for changes in baseball.

La Piña vs. La Peña

One of the most widely heard comments on the streets of Havana in 1997 was that the selection of *equipo Cuba* was not based upon *rendimiento* (performance), but on other factors, including favoritism. I heard over and over from fans that player selections were made by the baseball *piña.* Literally meaning "pineapple," *piña* refers to a small group—like the leaves tightly grouped together at the top of a pineapple—that makes decisions. *Piñas* exist throughout Cuban society, in governmental agencies, universities, and work centers. Cubans joke it's not so bad that a *piña* exists; it's just bad if you're not a member. Few players, however, found any humor in being left off *equipo Cuba* after having had a spectacular season.

Another complaint from fans was that Cuban baseball was being geared to a four-year cycle leading up to the Olympics. Thus, a player thought to be too old for the next Olympics may have been left off *equipo Cuba*, even though the numbers he put up during the year would seem to justify his inclusion. The case of Javier Méndez, an outfielder with the Industriales team in Havana, is a good example. "In all of the years that I have followed baseball and other sports, I don't know of any other athlete who has had such a formidable performance and not been selected," wrote sportswriter Capetillo when Méndez was not selected to the national team in 1997 after hitting .462.[6] Why was Méndez, who was thirty-three at the time, left off *equipo Cuba*?

"You'll have to ask them," Méndez told me in 1997, referring to the technical commission that selects the team. "The explanation given to me last year when I hit .462 was that I would be too old in 2000 for the Olympics. I'll be thirty-six." Méndez was selected—by the new commission—to *equipo Cuba* in 1998.

"Unfortunately, the case of Javier is not the only injustice in Cuban baseball," noted Capetillo, going on to cite several other examples from the 1980s and 1990s in which a player was not chosen for *equipo Cuba* even though his performance seemed to warrant it. Capetillo's remarks, coming a month before Cuba's loss in Barcelona, represented a popular consensus among Cuban fans and the views of many within the Cuban sports bureaucracy.

While there is no democratic structure for baseball fans to voice their displeasure over the selection of *equipo Cuba* or about the way the game is being run on the island, it is clear the government was aware of the level of popular discontent with the state of the game. The loss in Spain required the government to lay the blame on someone and to look seriously at the problems facing baseball. The government began to take action, but as will become clear, the policy changes would attack only part of the problem. There was little those in charge of charting the course of Cuban baseball could do about the country's larger economic problems, and nothing could push Fidel from his obsession with clinging to the amateur status of baseball.

Squeezed by the System

It doesn't make much difference whether you are the seventh best outfielder in Cuba if only six make the national team. The fact that baseball is the dominant sport in Cuba, combined with an excellent development system, produces a constant flow of quality players. But, because there are only a limited number of opportunities in the Cuban League and there is a significantly reduced opportunity to make the elite twenty-four-man *equipo Cuba*, many players do not advance. Quite simply, many younger players in Cuba are not developing their potential because of the long careers of veteran players.

Take the shortstop position for example. Americans have been fascinated by the New York Mets's Rey Ordóñez. But he was only a late-inning replacement for Germán Mesa—a true magician—on the Industriales team in Havana. A better example is Omar Linares. I asked Miguel Valdés in 1993 if he thought it was hard for some players to stay motivated when there was not likely to be an opening at their position—a situation rather like waiting for Jeff Bagwell, Barry Bonds, or Cal Ripken to retire. "I imagine Cuban players who play third base understand that there is little chance for them to play on *equipo Cuba*," said Valdés. "As long as Linares wants to play, they have few possibilities, because there is a superstar at that position."

"I remember when there was a proposal in the IBA [International Baseball Association] to end amateur status at age twenty-five," added Valdés. Although Cuba was opposed to the idea, Valdés did not think the age limit would have hurt Cuba's international team. "We would still be very strong. And further, the motivation would increase with the players we are developing. They might think, 'Well, Omar Linares is going to be twenty-five; maybe they will pick me to replace him.'"

Prior to 1995, retirement from Cuban baseball was almost identical to what occurs in the U.S. major leagues: a player, due to age or deteriorating skills, moves out of the game. I asked Valdés how the Cuban system deals with the transition for some of the stars of the game. He pointed out that while Lourdes Gourriel, the first baseman and sixteen-year veteran of *equipo Cuba* at that time, was thirty-six, he could still hit. Anticipating my next question, Valdés offered: "We have to begin to think about who will replace him. We have [Roberto] Colina, [Juan Carlos] Bruzón, [Juan Carlos] Millán. And a kid from Villa Clara, Jorge Luis Toca."

"You have to prepare a player for his retirement over a long period of time," explained Valdés. He said it is like talking to the family of someone who has a terminal illness. You talk about it so that when the person dies, the family is better prepared to deal with it. "But the player never understands that he has to retire. He will fight to keep playing."

Although the lack of advancement in baseball posed serious problems, an even more profound crisis confronted Cuban baseball and Cuban society in general. In the wake of the Soviet Union's collapse—and cut off from its natural trading partner, the United States—the bottom fell out of the Cuban economy in 1992. Cuban players, like everyone else in the country, had to struggle to put enough food on the dinner table.

In an effort to salvage the economy in 1993, Cuban President Fidel Castro allowed U.S. dollars to circulate.

No Cuban can live on monthly wages. Cuban baseball players receive only a small salary, less than $30 a month, but it takes an estimated $120 to meet basic necessities in Havana and just a bit less in the provinces. To help make ends meet, many Cuban families receive dollars from family and friends in the United States. University professors tend bar, medical doctors drive taxis, dentists sell wood carvings to tourists in Habana Vieja, families open their homes as restaurants or rent rooms, and prostitution—once a symbol of the corrupt regime of dictator Fulgencio Batista—is thriving. Some Cuban artists and writers are allowed to live in Mexico—the "velvet exile"—and return to Cuba whenever they like, and they are not branded as traitors. Cuban musical groups such as Los Van Van can play in Europe, South America, or the United States, earn hard currency, and return home.

A joke in Havana shortly after dollars began to circulate had a man going up to a bar and announcing that he was buying drinks for everyone. His wife rushes in and tells the bartender to stop. Her husband had a delusion that he was a taxi driver, she explained, when in reality he was only a neurosurgeon.

While the introduction of dollars may have helped resuscitate the Cuban economy, it has led to growing tension within Cuban society. Divisions between those who have access to dollars and those who do not have become very pronounced. This includes baseball players, who have no options. They can't live on their salaries, and Cuba's elite players, once the pampered children of the Revolution with access to special privileges, are effectively excluded from receiving dollars accessible to other Cubans. They have gone from having a special status to being an underprivileged group.[7] "A doctor can get another doctor to cover his shift while he goes to his job as a waiter," a fan in Havana pointed out, "But a ballplayer can't say, 'Hey, would you play first base while I go do something else to earn dollars?'"

The Rent-a-Coach Program and the Early Retirement of Players

Although it could not pay its players, INDER did find a way of rewarding retired sports figures, as well as financing many of its sports programs at home. In 1992, the Cuban government began a program that allowed coaches to work overseas and bring home a portion of their salary. In early 1999, there were just over six hundred Cuban coaches in thirty-six countries; about one-third of these coaches were baseball instructors, including many former members of *equipo Cuba.*

The seventy Cuban trainers and coaches in Italy were reported by the Cuban press as having "Cubanized" Italian baseball. Cubans again became missionaries of the game, a role they played throughout the Caribbean late in the nineteenth century.[8] Although 80 percent of the salaries earned goes to Cubadeportes, the branch of INDER that arranges the contracts, coaches retain the other 20 percent of their earnings.

In an effort to confront the desperate economic situation, to increase opportunities for younger players, and to stem defections, the Cuban government in 1996 allowed players over age thirty to retire and play overseas. About seventy players, including former national team stars Víctor Mesa, Lázaro Valle, and Pedro Luis Rodríguez, all of whom were still performing very well and who were huge fan favorites at home, retired. Although their playing days in Cuba were over, they went to semi-pro leagues in Japan, Italy, Nicaragua, Colombia, and El Salvador. As in the case of the contracts for coaches going overseas, Cubadeportes arranged the players' contracts, obtained visas, made travel arrangements, secured housing—and retained 80 percent of the earnings. The government share was used to finance sports programs in Cuba, including buying uniforms for all physical education teachers on the island. With the dollars they earned, players were able to "resolve" some of the financial difficulties they confronted.

A few Cuban baseball players had gone to Japan in 1994 and 1995, including outfielders Javier Méndez and Víctor Mesa and infielder Gabriel Pierre. They were not forced to "retire," but were allowed to return to play in Cuba.[9] Playing in Japan was clearly a positive experience for them. At the all-star game in Ciego de Ávila in 1998, I saw Méndez and Pierre go into the stands to welcome a delegation from the Japanese amateur baseball federation. Each player bowed and greeted their former managers in Japanese.

When news of the retirements first leaked out, the *Miami Herald* announced that "Havana is sending 50 top players to compete in Japan's industrial leagues [amateur leagues financed by Japanese companies]."[10] I asked Barros for more details on the players going overseas. "Fifty players did not go to Japan; it was probably not more than fifteen," explained Barros. Then he meticulously recalled from memory the name of each of the fifteen players, including Víctor Mesa and Lourdes Gourriel, who went to Japan in 1996.

"But players also went to Colombia, El Salvador, Ecuador, Italy, and Nicaragua," said Barros. In 1996, six Cubans played in Nicaragua, five in Italy, ten each in Ecuador and El Salvador, and thirty-six in Colombia. There were only six teams in the Colombian league, and all were managed by Cubans. In total, approximately eighty-five players went overseas. Commented Barros, "Older players like it because they can go to El Salvador and play, stay in shape, and bring home a few hundred dollars for their families. And here in Cuba, it opens space for younger players. It offers them more opportunities."

I mentioned to Barros that baseball was promoted in Central America in the early 1960s by the United States via the Alliance for Progress, part of an effort to curtail Cuban influence. It is ironic that the baseball programs that have languished in Central America for the past three decades are now being revived in part with Cuban assistance.

Speaking of the fifteen players who went to Asia, Barros said, "Players find it more difficult to go to Japan. It means six months away from your family in a very different culture with unusual food. Some players would rather go to Italy where the language and culture is not so different. Also in Japan they train a lot and play little," said Barros. "Cuban players would rather play a lot and train little."

While many players wanted to go overseas, Cuban fans saw their favorite teams decimated and were understandably unhappy with the retirement policy. During the two-year period between 1996 and 1998, the Provincia Habana team lost the first five batters in its lineup to retirement. And once retired, players were no longer eligible for selection to the national team.

"The players are happy with retirement, the fans are not," said Barros in 1997. "The problem is not that players are retiring; it is that so many players are retiring at one time. That is difficult to explain to the fans." "It was never explained to us," one caller complained on the radio call-in program *Deportavimente*. "We woke up one day and they were gone."

"Retirement was either a bad plan or a good plan that was not explained well," *Deportavimente* producer Pedro Cruz González told me.

"Ninety-nine percent of the calls we get on the subject are against the policy." And in his analysis of the loss in Barcelona in 1997, Carlos Cayetano wrote, "One of the most costly mistakes was to encourage veteran ball players—at the peak of their careers—to say good-bye to Cuban baseball."[11]

Even more disturbing were widely believed rumors in Cuba in 1997 that some players were tanking it so that they would be passed over for consideration for *equipo Cuba* and thus be allowed to go overseas and earn dollars for their families. It would make sense, and I have no doubt that some players did play poorly in order to be allowed to retire.

Although the retirement policy did facilitate the development and advancement of younger players and allow older players to earn money, the policy clearly was leading to a decline in the quality of baseball in Cuba.

Cuadros in the *Cuadro*

In December 1997, I noticed a young man wearing an INDER shirt seated just behind home plate at the Estadio Latinoamericano. In the first inning, Villa Clara pitcher Jorge Pérez was called for a balk and expressed his displeasure. The umpire took a couple of steps toward the pitcher's mound, but went no further and the incident was quickly over.

The new INDER man turned and asked the person seated next to him, "What's the pitcher's name?" The young baseball official may have been one of the few people in the ballpark who didn't know who Jorge Pérez was. "Jorge Pérez is not a rookie, and even if he was, it wouldn't make any difference," a fan leaned over to tell me. "How could he not know his name? Just seeing this tells you a lot about the current state of baseball in Cuba."

I'd heard that the government, concerned with the declining state of baseball and with an ongoing investigation concerning misuse of funds in INDER, was turning to *cuadros*—cadres.[12] INDER is considered to be among the most politically rigid of the Cuban government ministries. Although it is in charge of all sports, its number one priority is to defend the gains of the Revolution. When the Cuban system confronts a crisis in any area, it attempts to solve it by sending in someone who is a *cuadro*—a person grounded in the ideals of the Revolution. A new director had just been appointed at INDER, Humberto Rodríguez, age thirty-eight and a member of the Central Committee of the Communist Party for the past six years.

A Cuban friend explained that the idea of *cuadros* in Cuba was first articulated by Cuban revolutionary hero Ernesto "Che" Guevara. According to Che, in an article written in 1962, a *cuadro* is an individual who has reached a high enough level of political development to be able to interpret the *grandes directivas* that come from the central power. He is an individual with ideological and administrative discipline, "who would give his life for the Revolution." In short, a leader. "The *cuadro* is the core of the ideological motor of the Revolution." He keeps alive the spirit of the Revolution.[13] Che's article didn't mention baseball.

In essence, the baseball *cuadros* are disciples who interpret the theology of the Cuban Revolution. But placing *cuadros* in the *cuadro*— which also refers to a baseball diamond in Cuba—could not completely resolve baseball's problems, which are integrally linked to the crisis in Cuban economics, society, and politics. In an earlier time, the crisis in baseball would have been very important, but with the poor sugar harvest, power shortages, a rising crime rate, and a dozen other issues, it does not top the priority list.

One of the first actions taken by the new *cuadros en el cuadro* was to pay attention to the criticisms of the Cuban baseball fans. From the questions on radio talk shows to the constant chatter in the *esquinas calientes* throughout Cuba, it was clear that Cuban baseball fans had two fundamental demands: they wanted to see a quality product if they were going to make the sacrifice necessary to attend the games, and they wanted the selection of *equipo Cuba* to be based on the performance of the players during the regular season.

How would Cuban baseball officials deal with the overwhelming problems facing the national sport? I recalled the words of a secretary at INDER when I visited their offices in 1992 in search of a Cuban baseball cap. After I had been sent back and forth across Havana and had still come up empty-handed, the secretary told me that finding a cap, "*Será difícil* [will be difficult]." "Difficult or impossible?" I asked. "*Nada es imposible* [Nothing is impossible]," she responded with a sort of smile that implied otherwise. In 1997, INDER found it difficult to revive Cuban baseball, and by the end of the year, Cuba's baseball fans had turned their attention to the World Series and homegrown hero Liván Hernández. Both the fans and the Cuban government wondered which player would be the next to leave.

6 ☆ The Defectors

"It's not premeditated. Those who think about it [defecting] twice don't do it," Larry Rodríguez told me as we sat in the stands in Legion Park in Great Falls, Montana. Rodríguez had gone to Holland, Belgium, and Spain with a Cuban baseball team and returned home. But a few months later, when his Cuba B team [Cuba's second national team] traveled to Venezuela in October 1995, he and teammate Vladimir Núñez decided to remain behind. "If you are outside of Cuba and you want to stay, you stay."

On this windy June evening in Montana, with the temperature in the low forties, it was difficult to imagine the heat of a Cuban summer as Rodríguez and I spoke—only eight months after he made his decision to defect. Rodríguez, from Artemisa, about an hour's drive west of Havana, had pitched the night before and this night was charting the pitches (listing the type and speed of the pitches) for his Lethbridge, Alberta, team in the rookie Pioneer League game. I handed Rodríguez an umbrella as a light mist began to fall and went to get us both hot chocolate. When I returned, Rodríguez held the umbrella in one hand and had a pencil in the other with a clipboard on his lap. He had given his radar gun to my son Jorge, then eleven, having explained how to read it. For the rest of the game, Jorge would aim the gun at the pitcher and then hold it up for Rodríguez to record the velocity.

A wonderfully warm and energetic young man, Rodríguez speaks Spanish so rapidly that I sometimes had to listen to my tape recording half a dozen times afterward to completely understand him. During the course of our conversation, I explained that Great Falls derives its name from the waterfalls on the Missouri River just a few hundred yards from the ballpark. "Didn't the United States have a battleship Missouri?" asked Rodríguez. The Cubans do a good job of teaching U.S. history, I thought. "How did you know that?" I asked. "I saw it in a Steven Seagal film," he replied.

Rodríguez put most of the $1.3 million bonus money he received from the Arizona Diamondbacks in the bank, bought a BMW and a new home in Venezuela, and insists the money did not really change who he is and what he wants to achieve. The cash did, however, give him peace of mind about his future and his ability to help his family in Cuba. He doesn't waste time thinking about what might have been in Cuba. He has a great love for his homeland, but he also had long dreamed of playing in the United States.

In his three years in the Arizona Diamondback's minor league system, Rodríguez has struggled, compiling a 13–21 record while never pitching above Class A. After missing most of the 1998 season due to an injury, Rodríguez had surgery, but it did not correct the problem in his pitching arm. He would miss the entire 1999 season, and his major league dreams would be put on hold.

"The Most Beautiful Word Is Homeland"

As you approach Artemisa, a community of fifty thousand, the roadside is lined with monuments honoring local men killed in a major battle at the outset of the Cuban Revolution in 1953. Artemisa was not just another town that contributed young men to the cause. It provided the core group that attacked the Moncada Barracks in the eastern city of Santiago to initiate the armed struggle against the Batista dictatorship. Fidel Castro chose this close-knit group because of their ability to work together clandestinely. The list of the martyrs at Moncada numbers over fifty, fourteen of whom are from Artemisa.

Larry Rodríguez was not a well-known figure in Cuban baseball, but stop anyone in Artemisa and they will speak proudly of their native son. I did not ask Rodríguez for his family's address, nor did I ask anyone in Havana. I just assumed I would see kids playing sandlot ball and start a conversation that would lead to Rodríguez's family. When I found no one at the baseball park, I decided to ask a man standing on a street corner. "I used to play ball with Larry," said Fidel Hernández. "He is a really great person, and he has a good fastball. If you go back a few blocks towards the center of town, you will find his family's house."

The modest apartment where Rodríguez grew up is on the top floor of a two-story cinder-block building, just off the main highway. The new furniture and refrigerator in the apartment are recent gifts from Rodríguez. His father died when he was a child, and his mother now lives in another city closer to Havana.

"We are very proud of him," says his aunt, Caridad Valdés. "He sends photos and he calls us all the time to see how we are doing, but it's not the same. We can't see the expression on his face," she says. "Larry was born with a glove on his hand, and he grew up playing baseball in the street out front. He was a good student, but when he could escape from school, he would go play baseball. They all thought he was crazy."

Rodríguez's grandmother, Alejandra "Tín" Suárez, and grandfather, Ordulio Valdés, now in his mid-nineties, are delighted to have news of the young man they helped raise. They beam proudly as they look at a 1997 Topps baseball card featuring Rodríguez and fellow Diamondback Vladimir Núñez. Núñez hails from Guanajay, a small town less than ten miles from Artemisa. Even though they didn't know each other growing up, Rodríguez and Núñez decided to leave Cuba at the same time and ended up in the same organization.

· "I would like to go visit Larry for two or three months, and then come back to Cuba," said his grandfather. "I just don't want to go on a raft."

"It means leaving all of that behind—your friends, your childhood, aunts, uncles, brothers, everything—to come here, by yourself, and to struggle in a different world to try to reach a point where you can be successful and help your family," Rodríguez told me in Great Falls. "It is very difficult, and I have been very lucky."

"I have always loved baseball. They say a Cuban who does not know how to play baseball is not a Cuban. I began playing organized ball when I was eleven," said Rodríguez. "When I lost a game, I did not sleep. When I won and didn't play well, I did not sleep." It was that intensity and love for the game that earned Rodríguez Rookie of the Year honors in Cuban baseball in the 1994–1995 season. But despite his outstanding performance, he was almost unknown in Cuba, partly because he had a meteoric rise and played for a team outside the capital that received little press coverage.

Unlike Vladimir Núñez, who was one of the rising stars in Cuban baseball, having been selected three times to the Cuban junior national team, Rodríguez was not a prospect. Rodríguez entered organized Cuban baseball as an outfielder and converted to pitcher at age fourteen. While he threw hard, he had control problems. Finally, he was told to go into the military, something no prospect in the Cuban system is required to do. "Military service for me was like retirement. But when I came back from the military, I was another person," said Rodríguez. He began the 1994–95 season on the Provincia Habana team in the Serie de Desarrollo, pitched well, was brought up to the main team, compiled a 7–3 record, and emerged as one of Cuba's top pitching prospects.

"Larry Rodríguez became Rookie of the Year, and then he left. Most people in Cuba would not remember him. We didn't see Larry because he played on a team from Havana province, not one of the teams from the city," said Barros. "I'm not sure that Larry ever pitched a televised game in Cuba." After reading an article I wrote about my trip to Artemisa, Rodríguez called me in early 1998.[1] "Remind Sigfredo when you see him that I was on television during the playoffs," he said. "He knows that I was pitching because he was at the game." A month later I relayed the message to Barros, and his only response was a sheepish grin.

Along the same highway from Artemisa to Havana that Rodríguez took to begin his journey toward a career in major league baseball, there are the ever-present billboards with political slogans. "Each generation has its hour and its work to do," reads one. Another announces; "The most beautiful word is homeland." Larry Rodríguez would agree with both. But the path that Rodríguez chose to leave his homeland was forged by another Cuban player four years earlier.

The First Defector: René Arocha

In July 1991, René Arocha, a pitcher on *equipo Cuba*, decided not to board his return flight to Cuba from Miami. Two days before his decision to remain in the United States, I had spoken with Arocha in Millington, Tennessee, where the Cuban team played a four-game exhibition against Team USA. Had I paid closer attention, I might have noticed that he did not buy a small electric fan at K-Mart to take back to Cuba as did most other players.

"I remember the first desertion of a Cuban player after the Revolution, René Arocha," said Gilberto Dihigo. "When he signed a big league contract, people in Cuba began to follow his career—not his team—because they were not interested in the St. Louis Cardinals, but they began to follow *el cubano*. For me, Arocha's leaving was a dagger in the heart for the regime, because Arocha showed the other players that they could also leave. At this time there were only a few sports figures who had defected."

"*Empieza el cosquilleo de 'yo puedo'* [Then the 'I can do it too' attitude began]," explained Dihigo. This response, he said, was a natural desire on the part of baseball players to compete at the highest level and was not a political statement. This fact, he believed, was something the Cuban government was incapable of understanding.

"For a long time the siege mentality of Cubans who remember the Batista years and who supported Castro's revolution in the face of North American hostility was sufficient to keep the nation's top athletes loyal to the Cuban flag. However, more than thirty years after the revolution, with the economy in tatters, it seems that patriotism alone is an insufficient guarantee that Cuban athletes will remain fully committed to the revolution, and defection has emerged as a serious problem for Cuban sport," writes John Sugden in his study of Cuban boxing.[2]

In Spanish, the verb *desertar* (to defect) has a military connotation, and many fans in Cuba prefer not to use it. In the United States, the word *defection* conjures images of people trying to escape over the Berlin Wall while dodging bullets fired by border guards. Although New York Yankees pitcher Orlando "El Duque" Hernández did take a risk by fleeing the island by boat to the Bahamas in late 1997, most of the forty or so Cuban baseball players who have made the decision to pursue their professional dreams outside of Cuba did not take such drastic measures. Cuban teams frequently compete outside of the country, and a player can walk away at almost any time. In the official record books, any player no longer in Cuba has an asterisk by his name. The explanation simply states *abandonó el país* (left the country).

"They think we have the players tied to the beds in their rooms when we go overseas. It's just not true," explained Miguel Valdés. "The players go and do what they want." I stayed in the same motel with the Cuban team in Millington in 1991 and 1993. I saw players walk over to K-Mart, to the grocery store, and to the ballpark. For them, the physical act of defecting was relatively easy. But the actual decision for a Cuban player to leave his country is wrenching. While most U.S. sportswriters focus on what a Cuban player can gain by defecting, including an opportunity to play and earn millions of dollars, few in the United States are aware of what a player has to lose by leaving Cuba.

Defection implies a rejection of *patria* (homeland), and in Cuba defectors are often branded as helping the enemy by selling out their country. But their reasons for leaving are not primarily political; they are a reflection of the lack of professional advancement at home and the country's severe economic crisis that began in the early 1990s.

"This is a very difficult decision. It is not at all easy," Arocha told me as we sat in the Astrodome's visiting dugout watching fireworks after a Fourth of July weekend game in 1993. "You have to have an inner strength—it's incredible the strength you have to have to leave behind not only your family—although leaving your family is difficult—but to leave your roots, something that is yours, and to understand that you don't know when you will be able to return." As we spoke it was clear he really missed the companionship of some of the players on *equipo Cuba*. "During spring training in St. Petersburg, I listened to Radio Rebelde from Cuba and heard a game in the Serie Selectiva between Habana and the Occidentales," explained Arocha.

And while Arocha is interested in Cuba, the Cubans—even government officials who proclaim him a traitor—ask about him and wish him well. His success is in part a tribute to the baseball development system in Cuba.

Arocha's defection came as a surprise not only to the Cuban government, but to most major league teams in the United States and to the Office of the Commissioner as well, which ruled that he would be subject to a special draft to determine which team would have the right to sign him. And although former big league pitcher and Cuban native Pedro Ramos said Arocha "has the potential of Nolan Ryan," not all clubs were excited. "We saw him pitch. He was [Cuba's] third or fourth pitcher. He is not one of their aces. There is not a tremendous amount of interest in him," said Gary Hughes, now assistant general manager of the Colorado Rockies, then scouting director with the Montreal Expos.

TABLE 2
Ages of Selected Cuban Defectors

René Arocha
Date defected: July 1991
Place: Miami, Florida
Birth date claimed in United States: February 24, 1966
Cuban age: A 1991 Cuban roster lists his age as twenty-seven, which would put his birth year as 1964. A 1980 newspaper article seems to confirm this earlier date. A January 2, 1980 article in *Granma* mentions a fifteen-year-old René Arocha pitching in the Serie Nacional. If Arocha was actually born in February 1966, he would have been thirteen at the time. In fact, only two players have played in the Serie Nacional at age fifteen: Arocha is one of them. No one has played at a younger age.

Rolando Arrojo
Date defected: July 9, 1996
Place: Albany, Georgia
Birth date claimed in United States: July 18, 1968
Cuban age: Cuban records list Arrojo's date of birth as May 29, 1964. His Cuban baseball card has the same date, both of which correspond to his passport and documents submitted to the U.S. State Department to obtain his visa in 1996. If the 1968 date is correct, he began playing in the Serie Nacional when he was only fifteen, but this is not likely.

Liván Hernández
Date defected: September 27, 1995
Place: Monterrey, Mexico
Birth date claimed in United States: February 20, 1975
Cuban age: Cuban records also list the February 20, 1975, birth date for Liván.

Orlando Hernández
Date defected: December 26, 1998
Place: Left Cuba by boat, landed in the Bahamas
Birth date claimed in United States: October 11, 1969
Cuban age: Cuban records list Orlando Hernández's date of birth as October 10, 1965. Numerous interviews in Cuba seem to confirm this date as accurate, rather than the younger age claimed by "El Duque."

Rey Ordóñez
Date defected: 1993
Place: Buffalo, New York
Birth date claimed in United States: November 11, 1972
Cuban age: Cuban records show Ordóñez's date of birth as January 11, 1971. This is an easy one. Ordóñez told a U.S. sportswriter his birth date is January 11, 1971.

Arocha played for the St. Louis Cardinals for three seasons (1993–1995) and compiled an 18–17 record. He did not play in 1996, was traded to the San Francisco Giants in 1997, and in 1998 pitched for a few months at New Orleans, the Houston Astros Triple A affiliate. Then Arocha, who began his career as one of the youngest players in the Serie Nacional at age fifteen, decided after eighteen seasons to retire.[3] After several bad outings in June 1998, Arocha told New Orleans pitching coach Jim Hickey that he was having problems retiring the same batters that he had struck out earlier in the season. He was tired and did not want to undergo surgery or rehabilitation. Hickey told him to take a few weeks off and rethink his decision, but Arocha chose to retire. "I bet a couple of million pitches came out of that arm," Hickey told me.[4]

"Once René did it and survived, our decision was made," says Iván Alvarez, a pitcher who, along with outfielder Alexis Cabreja and infielder Osmani Estrada, left their Industriales team during a tournament in Mérida, Mexico, in September 1992.[5] They flew to Mexico City, lay low because they were fearful Mexicans authorities might return them to Cuba, and continued on to the border city of Tijuana, where they reportedly just walked over to the United States.

Arriving in Los Angeles, the three went to the house of a Cuban American businessman and part-time agent, Gus Domínguez, who also represented René Arocha. They did not seek political asylum, and they asked the Commissioner's office to consider them as free agents, making them free to negotiate contracts with any major league organization. Nonetheless, the position outlined by Domínguez foreshadowed the maneuver that agent Joe Cubas would use a few years later to negotiate multimillion-dollar contracts for other Cuban defectors. These three players, however, did not have Arocha's stature. None had played on *equipo Cuba*, and Major League Baseball turned down their claim.[6]

Alvarez, Cabrera, and Estrada did not find the dream they had hoped for. Cabrera and Estrada both signed with the Texas Rangers. Estrada had the most success, eventually making it to Triple A, and he was still playing there in 1998, before going to Taiwan.

On July 12, 1993, Rey Ordóñez, shortstop for Cuba B, defected while playing in the World University Games in Buffalo, New York.[7] The New York Mets acquired his rights in a special lottery, gave him a $100,000 bonus, and waited for him to get to the big leagues. Of the approximately forty Cuban players who defected between 1991 and

TABLE 3
Cuban Defectors: Comparisons of U.S. and Cuban Statistics

	Seasons	Games	Won-Lost	Percentage	Innings	BB	K	ERA
René Arocha								
Cuba	11	245	104–72	.591	1412.2	544	1038	3.18
MLB	3	118	18–17	.514	320.2	70	183	3.87
Rolando Arrojo								
Cuba	13	359	154–98	.611	2027.2	442	1138	3.50
MLB	1	32	14–12	.538	202	65	152	3.56
Liván Hernández								
Cuba	3	49	27–16	.628	335	127	311	4.57
MLB	3	51	19–15	.558	333.2	144	236	4.23
Orlando Hernández								
Cuba	10	246	126–47	.728	1514.1	455	1211	3.05
MLB	1	21	12–4	.750	141	52	131	3.13

	Seasons	Games	Avg.	Bats	Hits	2B	3B	HR	RBI	BB	K
Rey Ordóñez											
Cuba	4	272	.261	712	186	23	4	4	71	23	76
MLB	3	424	.242	1363	330	37	9	3	105	63	149

1998, Ordóñez is the only position player to make it to the major leagues, where his outstanding fielding earned him Gold Gloves in 1997, 1998, and 1999.

"Germán Mesa back in Cuba says, 'Y yo qué? [What about me?] I'm better than Ordóñez. I'm a better hitter, I run better, and I field better. If I went to the big leagues, I could do it; I could play at that level,'" says Dihigo. "Ordóñez couldn't hold a candle to Germán Mesa."

Ordóñez was not the first player to defect from the Cuba team during the World University Games. On July 10, two days before Ordóñez left, Edilberto Oropeza, a left-handed pitcher, jumped a fence in Niagara Falls, New York, before a game. "Arocha is our inspiration," announced Oropeza at the time. Oropeza, a 6'3", 215-lb. left-handed pitcher has had success in six minor league seasons but has yet to make it to the big leagues.

Most defector lists don't include Euclides Rojas, but he was the closer on *equipo Cuba* for more than five years. In fact, Rojas made more relief appearances than any other pitcher in post-1959 baseball in Cuba, and is the country's all-time save leader.[8] And while many think Orlando Hernández was the first to leave in a boat, it was actually Rojas who left Cuba on a homemade raft with his wife and son in August of 1994, embarking on a journey he hoped would take him to the United States. Instead, he was picked up by the U.S. Coast Guard and, because of an immigration agreement between Cuba and the United States, was taken to the U.S. naval base at Guantánamo, Cuba, where he was held for six months before being allowed to go to the United States.

Rojas pitched with Palm Springs in the independent leagues (leagues not affiliated with Major League Baseball organizations), and then played in the minor leagues for the Florida Marlins. On June 2, 1996, he was released by the Marlins and hired by the club as a pitching coach on the same day. The Marlins 1998 Media Guide lists him as thirty, but he is really three or four years older.

Two younger players, left-handed pitcher Michael Tejera and right-hander Hanzel Izquierdo, both members of the Cuban junior national team, defected in Miami in 1994 and attended high school there. Both were selected by the Florida Marlins in the 1995 June draft and played two years in the Gulf Coast Rookie League. In 1999, Tejera made it to the major leagues with the Marlins, while Izquierdo, released from the Marlins after two seasons, is considered a big league prospect with the Chicago White Sox.

1995: Enter Joe Cubas, Midwife to the Defectors

"No Mafia or CIA master-minded plot to overthrow Fidel Castro has worked as efficiently to gnaw at the foundations of the Cuban Communist regime as the clandestine missions of baseball agent Joe Cubas to transport freedom-seeking baseball players to the United States, and secure them some of the largest contracts in amateur baseball history," wrote Joe Cubas, age thirty-eight, in the introduction to his book proposal *Sliding into Freedom.*

He may be right. Not only did the presence of the Miami-based agent wherever *equipo Cuba* played (except inside Cuba) drive Cuban authorities crazy, but the fact that he was able to secure multimillion-dollar bonuses by circumventing the U.S. amateur draft was alluring to Cuban players. There is no question that Joe Cubas changed the way

Major League Baseball would deal with Cuban players. Ironically, if the United States were to end the embargo, Cubas would just be another agent.

While Cubas's desire to politically embarrass the Castro government seems paramount, he's become very wealthy in the process. Cubas claims to have undergone severe economic hardships to carry out his operations, but he has certainly been rewarded, even if he only took a 5 percent commission off the bonuses of the multimillion-dollar contracts of Osvaldo Fernández, Liván Hernández, Larry Rodríguez, Vladimir Núñez, Rolando Arrojo, and Orlando Hernández. He has vigorously denied reports he took a higher percentage, but Liván Hernández, Rodríguez, and Núñez all left Cubas and hired new agents within a year of arriving in the United States.

Cubas exaggerates the intrigue surrounding many of the defections, lowers the age of the players, and often inflates their capabilities.[9] While there is no question Cubas has aided some outstanding players, he often touts any Cuban male under the age of thirty who can walk and chew gum at the same time as a prospect. Scouts flocked to see Roberto Colina, William Ortega, and Jesús Ametller at a try-out camp in Florida in early 1997 because they were Cuban. If they had been Dominican or Venezuelan, no scouts would have shown up to see what are essentially players with a minor league ceiling.

"Cubas—who fancies himself part sports agent, part secret agent—spends a considerable amount of time looking over his shoulder. Never mind the fact no one's there," wrote *Los Angeles Times* writer Kevin Baxter in one of the few serious journalistic articles about Cubas.[10] It is doubtful that Cubas had to evade Mexican authorities to bring players to safety or that the players who left by boat were not part of some elaborate smuggling operation, but Cubas's stories fit right into the last remaining skirmish of the Cold War. If they were true, they would be the stuff movies are made of. In fact, there is a movie proposal currently being shopped around Hollywood. Joe Cubas, known as *el gordo* (the fat man), claims that in the film he will be played by Antonio Banderas. It's a stretch, but precise details have not been one of Joe Cubas's strong points.[11]

Joe Cubas did, however, successfully challenge the Major League Baseball rule that Cuban defectors must enter the U.S. amateur draft. Cubas took his players to a third country—first the Dominican Republic and then Costa Rica—where he had arranged for their residency. Then, as in the case with other players not living in the United States, Canada, or Puerto Rico, the Cubans could negotiate with the highest bidder. Playing off the Cuban players' exoticism, Cubas was able to obtain multimillion-dollar bonuses for his clients. Just as Cuban cigars, sometimes with their identifying bands removed, are smuggled into the United States from Mexico or Canada, Cuban baseball players were being repackaged in the Dominican Republic and Costa Rica for sale in the United States.

The first defector to sign with Cubas was Osvaldo Fernández, who simply walked away from the team motel in Millington on July 30, 1995. In September of the same year, Liván Hernández left the Cuban team in Monterrey, Mexico. Cubas, after arranging their residency in the Dominican Republic, took both players, now free agents, on a dog-and-pony show to several major league stadiums and waited for the bids to come in. In January 1996, Hernández signed a $4.5-million contact with the Marlins, which included a $2.5-million bonus. Fernández received $3.2 million for a three-year deal with the San Francisco Giants. In 1995, pitchers Vladimir Núñez and Larry Rodríguez defected and because of their age—they were both twenty-one at the time—attracted a great deal of attention from major teams, resulting in large bonuses for the two.

By 1996, Joe Cubas was announcing that he would charter a Greyhound bus to accommodate the Cuban players who would defect at the Atlanta Olympics. But because only Rolando Arrojo decided to remain in the United States, the bus was unnecessary. Arrojo, who had dominated the U.S. Olympic team in an exhibition game only ten days before, left the team when *equipo Cuba* was in Albany, Georgia, on July 9. Cubas reportedly just knocked on the door of Arrojo's room at the team hotel, and the two left together. Albany police said that no effort was made to guard the Cuban players and that they were free to move about. Although he could wander about easily, Arrojo's next decision was more arduous. "It was a very hard decision, but I had to make it to achieve my dream of gaining freedom and playing in the major leagues," Arrojo told the *Miami Herald*. "I'm a little unhappy right now. I'm sorry I didn't tell my teammates, but it was a very personal decision and I had to make it all by myself."

Arrojo established his residency in Costa Rica and, in April of 1997, signed a contract with the Tampa Bay Devil Rays for $7 million. In 1998, Arrojo went 14–12, was selected to play in the All-Star Game, and was a leading candidate to be the American League Rookie of the Year.

My friends at the Peña back in Havana could not understand why he was passed over for the honor, which was given to Oakland outfielder Ben Grieve.

Liván Hernández: The First Successful Defector

When Liván Hernández beat the Atlanta Braves while allowing only three hits on October 12, 1996, in the National League Championship Series, baseball fans in the United States got a glimpse of what awaits once the United States and Cuba reestablish formal diplomatic relations. Hernández is the real thing, the first of the Cuban defectors to have an impact on major league baseball.

I first wrote about Liván Hernández in 1992 when, as a seventeen-year-old, he pitched a no-hitter for the Cuban junior team in Monterrey, Mexico. Coincidentally, just three years later in September 1995, Hernández would walk away while *equipo Cuba* was in Monterrey for an exhibition series. Within a year, he would pitch his first game in the major leagues with the Florida Marlins.

When Hernández dropped agent Joe Cubas, no reason was given for the separation, although it was rumored that it was related to the amount of the cut Cubas took from Liván's bonus, a point no one wanted to discuss. Not surprisingly, in early 1997 Cubas was telling reporters that Hernández was overweight and out of shape. Hernández admits having difficulty passing up a McDonald's during his year and a half in the minor leagues, but that was to be expected for a young, strapping man just arrived from Cuba, where he had had neither money for nor access to fast food restaurants.

In February 1997, I ran into Gary Hughes, then Marlins Vice President, and asked him if Liván was indeed overweight. "He looks great to us," replied Hughes. He thought Liván was right on track to pitch in the major leagues later that year. Brought up from the minor leagues in June, Hernández won nine consecutive games before finishing with a 9–3 record. In the National League Championship Series, Hernández won a game in relief against the Atlanta Braves, and then in the same weekend, made an unexpected start and struck out a post-season-record fifteen batters on his way to a complete game victory against the Braves. Very few pitchers beat Atlanta twice in the same weekend. In the World Series, Hernández earned two victories over the Cleveland Indians and won the MVP award.

I asked Julio Sarmiento, of the Marlins public relations office and the one who translated for Liván during the World Series, to arrange an interview with Liván. I wanted to go to spring training and speak to him about his experiences as a baseball player in Cuba—but with no mention of politics, a subject I knew was taboo. Sarmiento told me Liván also did not want to talk about his defection.

In early January, *Baseball Weekly* asked me to go to Miami to interview Hernández for a cover story. I called Sarmiento, who said he would try to arrange an interview but that it wouldn't be easy. Liván was tired of talking to the press, said Sarmiento, and he shied away from interviews by saying he had to work out or he had a golf date. "The last time I went down to the training room, Liván asked, 'What do you want now?,'" added Sarmiento. Finally, with some prodding, Liván agreed to an interview.

In early February, I went to Pro Player Stadium and met with Julio. At the same time, I ran into an old friend from Venezuela, Adolfo Salguiero, who works in the Marlins Hispanic marketing department. For a while, Adolfo had served as Liván's translator in the minor leagues. "The way he performed in the World Series showed he can take the pressure on the mound. I have no doubt about that and I don't think that will ever change, " said Adolfo. "The part I'm not sure about is being a celebrity. Can he handle that? I guess we will find out," said Adolfo. "Good luck with your interview." In the Marlins clubhouse, I got my first sense of Liván's major league attitude. His surly demeanor was so different from the warm greeting I had received from René Arocha, Vladimir Núñez, and Larry Rodríguez, and from players in Cuba. Liván didn't want to do the interview but reluctantly agreed to meet at his condo in Miami Beach. It turned out to be the most difficult player interview I have ever done.

Liván Hernández was born in the province of Villa Clara but moved to Isla de la Juventud when he was five. His father, Arnoldo Hernández, also the father of Orlando "El Duque" Hernández, played in the Cuban League.

"My dad was a good pitcher, but he didn't teach me very much because my parents separated when I was very young," Hernández told me as we looked out of the balcony of his high-rise condo in Miami Beach. Liván began to play organized baseball when he was nine, was identified as a prospect, and went to the EIDE and ESPA on Isla de la Juventud. At seventeen, he began a two-year stint with the Cuban junior team and traveled to Monterrey, Mexico, and Windsor, Canada, then moved up to *equipo Cuba*.

He left the Cuban team in Mexico on September 27, 1995, and within one year, on September 24, 1996, made his major league debut. Although he thinks he paid his dues in the minors, he had less than one year there—363 days—before getting to the big leagues. Most young players from Latin America spend five or six years in the minors making the transition.

Liván Hernández would have little time to adjust to wooden bats, to developing more pitches and working on his location, and to facing batters who had more power than those he had confronted at the amateur level. He also had to adjust to a new country, a new language, and new foods. "It was a rapid change. But you have to adjust, little by little," explained Hernández. Still, he did not think it would be so rough. "You miss your family, the food, everything. Then there is the solitude. The life on the streets is much different here. In Cuba you have friends, and here you don't know anyone. I have a strong character. You have to overcome challenges."

On the diamond, he was successful. But he confronted a bigger challenge—*libertad*. He had come from Cuba, where he had no money and little freedom to act. Now, in the United States, he had more money than he could spend and the freedom to do just about anything he wanted. In Cuba he did not have to make many choices. Here he had to make too many.

I showed Hernández a 1994 Cuban baseball card of himself and asked what was the difference between the person in the photo and the person in front of me? "I was a bit skinnier in the photo," he replied with a laugh. But he was clearly taken aback. He had to think about Cuba. How does it feel to be a twenty-two-year-old who accomplishes what two years before he could have never dreamed of? I asked. "*No sé* [I don't know]." Thirty minutes into the interview, Hernández shut down and "*No sé*" was the response to almost any question. I asked how he felt after he struck out fifteen Atlanta Braves. "*No sé*." Was there a time last year when you finally realized that you had made it—that you really were a major league player? "*No sé*." Questions about Joe Cubas went unanswered, and the interview soon ended. Liván Hernández seemed to be a very talented, immature, and lonely young man.

The implications of Hernández's defection are stunning. He is the best product of Cuba's well-organized baseball system, and his success with the Marlins is a symptom of that system's disarray. Cuba lost its first international tournament in ten years in August 1997, and the Cuban people, including Fidel, followed every one of Hernández's pitches in the World Series—the first Cuban since Luis Tiant with the Boston Red Sox in 1975 to pitch in the fall classic. And certainly Fidel heard Hernández shout, "I love you, Miami" in English when he was awarded the MVP trophy.

When the defections are looked at one at a time, they don't seem to mean much, and attempting to evaluate the talent level in Cuba based on these defections is misleading. The vast majority of Cuba's quality baseball players have remained on the island. But Liván Hernández's standing on the mound before the opening game of the 1997 World Series, his brother Orlando's winning game two of the 1998 World Series, and the attention those events drew in Cuba is a clear portent that the desire for playing in the United States will surely spread in Cuba. A gold medal in the Olympics may no longer be enough— especially given the economic hardship players must endure in Cuba.

In July 1996, Liván's half-brother, Orlando Hernández, was detained by Cuban state security agents and grilled for twelve hours about his relationship to Juan Ignacio Hernández Nodar, a Cuban American player agent who had been arrested in Cuba with fake passports and with money sent by Liván for Orlando. In the past, Hernández Nodar had worked with his cousin, Joe Cubas, but Cubas insists Hernández Nodar broke off from him and was working on his own, and the Cuban government supported that claim in an official statement.[12] Two weeks later, Hernández Nodar was sentenced to fifteen years in prison, and the next day Orlando Hernández was told he would not be on the team going to the Atlanta Olympics. The reason: poor performance, although he had in fact been playing very well. In October 1996, Orlando Hernández, Germán Mesa, and Alberto Hernández, all of whom had played on *equipo Cuba*, were banned for life from Cuban baseball for accepting money from an agent.

In July 1997, when Eduardo Paret, shortstop on the gold medal team at the Atlanta Olympics, and two of his Villa Clara teammates, infielder Osmani García and catcher Angel López, spoke with Rolando Arrojo by telephone, they were banned from baseball for maintaining contact with *traidores al béisbol* (baseball traitors).

Although the Cuban government has little control over what its players do outside of Cuba, in coming down hard on the players it issued a warning to outside agents and scouts—don't mess with us on our turf. The bannings were a reminder that making money off baseball was still an activity reserved for the state.

In 1999, there were two more defections. In April, Bryan Peña, a seventeen-year-old catcher and member of the Cuban junior team, left during a tournament in Venezuela. In August, Danis Báez, a twenty-two-year-old right-handed pitcher, defected from *equipo Cuba* during the Pan American Games in Winnipeg. Joe Cubas held a tryout camp in Costa Rica in October for Báez, and on November 5 he signed a four-year, $14.5-million contract with the Cleveland Indians. They will not be the last players to defect.

7 ☆ The Defection of the Banned

Orlando "El Duque" Hernández had no choice but to get out of Cuba. He had been banned from baseball, and a pitcher not able to pitch is like a sugar cane cutter without a machete. I had naively thought the Cuban authorities might just give him an exit visa and let him leave. But with Livián's success, government officials came down harder on Orlando, making his life miserable and often bringing him in for questioning. Just weeks before his journey, "El Duque" had been told by Cuban state security that he would be sent to prison for even thinking about leaving the island. Marcelo Sánchez had joked about how Orlando had become "El Duquecito" (the little duke) because Livián was now "El Duque." Although he said it in jest, the sobriquet carried an ironic sadness—Orlando had been placed in the shadow of his younger brother.

The day after Christmas 1997, Hernández and seven others—including his girlfriend, Noris Bosch; Alberto Hernández, another banned player; and Joél Pedrozo, who claimed to be a ballplayer but was really just Orlando's cousin, left Cuba by boat and ended up in a detention center in the Bahamas. The circumstances of their departure from Cuba and arrival on a small deserted island in the Bahamas are murky. Although initial reports described a twenty-foot boat, within a few weeks many newspaper reports had him on a "leaky" boat, a "rickety sailboat," or an "unseaworthy vessel."[1] "If his agent thought Orlando was going to sign a multimillion-dollar contract, why would he risk his investment on a raft?" asked one Havana fan in disbelief when told of U.S. media reports on the defection.

"U.S. immigration officials said that in previous cases, Cubans with means have been smuggled out in larger vessels, then dropped off in small craft to await rescue, a method that minimizes the risk of the crossing and avoids detection of the smuggling operation," reported the *Washington Post* a few days after Orlando arrived in the Bahamas.[2] Coast Guard authorities also reported the Hernández group as being in "excellent condition," not what they normally encounter with groups that have spent four days on a deserted island.

The boat in which "El Duque" and his party departed Cuba was twenty feet long and moved along at twenty knots an hour. Its destination was Anguilla Cay in the Bahamas, a small island frequently used as a staging area for Cubans being smuggled to the United States. According to a *Sports Illustrated* story, the group was to be met by a boat sent from Miami. That boat encountered mechanical problems, and Hernández and his party were stranded for three days until they were spotted by a U.S. Coast Guard helicopter.[3]

If, in fact, Orlando Hernández was smuggled off the island by boat, he would be no different from hundreds of other Cubans who have used this method in recent years. "I haven't seen a real *balsero* [rafter] in months," Commander Jim McKenzie, U.S. Coast Guard liaison with Cuba, told the *Miami Herald*.[4] An official of the Border Patrol added, "The smugglers are carrying people who can afford to pay or are important." The going rate is about $8,000 per person.

But U.S. government authorities did not treat Orlando Hernández as they do the hundreds of other Cubans who depart from the island in boats each year and are apprehended outside of U.S. territory. After a lengthy debate within the Clinton administration, the U.S. government announced that it would grant political asylum to Orlando, Alberto Hernández, and Noris Bosch, but not the others in their group. Orlando Hernández declined, stating that if the others could not go to the United States, neither would he. Had Hernández accepted the U.S. offer of political asylum, he would have been subject to Major League Baseball's amateur draft. By going to a third country, he would be treated as a free agent and thus be able to negotiate a more lucrative contract.

Within a week of his arrival in the Bahamas, Orlando Hernández and the others were on their way to Costa Rica, where they would eventually be granted residency. By early February, Hernández would put on a exhibition for major league scouts. In early March, amid rumors of a joint baseball-movie deal with Disney's Anaheim Angels, he signed a four-year contract with the New York Yankees for $6.6 million. Fidel—although not mentioning Hernández by name—called him a *mercachifle* (a peddler or huckster) and a "mercenary of sports."

Although Joe Cubas claimed Hernández was twenty-eight, Cuban records had him at thirty-two. "And to those who say I'm thirty-two years old, not twenty-eight, all I can say is that when the time comes, I'll show on the playing field how good my arm is," was Hernández's only comment about his age. Another question mark was "El Duque's" long hiatus from the game. Would he be able to get himself into shape? By the time he signed, spring training was nearing an end and clearly it would be tough going. But Hernández had stayed in condition in Cuba. Sustained by his desire to once again play baseball, he had been running six miles a day in Havana and playing shortstop on his neighborhood team (he was too good to pitch). After only a few weeks in Florida, a Yankees team doctor pronounced Hernández the best-conditioned athlete he had ever seen.

"I would not be surprised if Orlando could stick around the big leagues for a few years," said U.S. player agent Jaime Torres, who had seen Hernández play on many occasions. "He does not have the blazing fastball of Rolando Arrojo, but "El Duque" knows how to pitch. He knows how to change speeds and he can spot his pitches. And he is mentally tough." One major league executive described Hernández as having the heart of a lion. A 1990 major league scouting report on "El Duque" indicated he had an above-average fastball, eighty-eight to ninety miles an hour, with good movement.

Although Hernández had Cuba's all-time winning percentage at .728 and a 126–47 record, he had to start at the bottom in the United States, and he happily reported to the Yankee farm club in the Florida State League. He went 1–0 at Class A Tampa, was undefeated with six victories at Triple A Columbus, and on June 3, 1998, made his major league debut at Yankee Stadium with a 7–1 win over Tampa Bay. He finished the year at 12–4 and 3.13 ERA. During the playoffs, he won a key game against Cleveland and then started and won game two in the Yankees four-game sweep of the San Diego Padres. His combined record for the year was 21–5.

The old scouting reports didn't say anything about his high leg kick, his unusual windup, and his ability to throw the ball from different angles that made it difficult for the batter to see his release point and made his fastball seem much faster. His style, both on and off the field, was refreshing. Here was a pitcher who was not afraid to throw inside, who was an outstanding fielder, and who was not apprehensive about talking to a reporter on his pitching day—something no U.S. pitcher will do.

And Hernández answered Fidel's jabs with one of his own: he said he enjoyed pitching on Sunday evenings because he knew the games were on national television and that the *comandante en jefe* would be watching from Cuba.

Sigfredo Barros recalls the first time Orlando Hernández pitched in Estadio Latinoamericano. "He came in relief in the first inning in a game against Pinar del Río with the bases loaded and gave up a home run to Luis Casanova. It was 1986 or 1987. Orlando Hernández is very smart and he works very hard," said Barros.

No one in Cuba, it seems, has anything unkind to say about Orlando Hernández. The Cuban news agency Prensa Latina even ran a short note about Hernández's victory in the World Series. There was no mention of his nationality.

It was clear during the season that although Orlando Hernández was an incredibly strong person, he sorely missed his children who had remained behind. "Castro says he is a human being. Why doesn't he prove it and let my family reunite?" Hernández commented while he was still in Costa Rica before signing with the Yankees. After an August game in Montreal, Hernández turned his chair to face his locker and cried. But only three months later, he was overjoyed when his two children, Yahumara, age eight, and Steffi, age three, along with his mother and ex-wife, were allowed to join him for the Yankees World Series victory celebration. Cardinal John O'Connor, using the small opening remaining from Pope John Paul II's visit to Cuba in January 1998, wrote to Fidel asking for visas for Hernández's family. "We are grateful to President Castro," said Cardinal O'Connor at the celebratory mass. Fidel was still able to use "El Duque" for his own political purposes.

But Orlando was clearly the winner in this match-up. In 1999, he won twenty-one games and became the ace of the Yankees staff. When he was awarded the American League post-season MVP trophy,

Orlando said, "This is for my teammates," and after a pause added, "and for Cuba." And at the *esquinas calientes* in Cuba, he was again being referred to as "El Duque."

Jorge Luis Toca and the Second Wave of the Banned

By late March 1998, the dust was beginning to settle from the defections of Orlando and Alberto Hernández. Orlando had signed with the New York Yankees, while Alberto was settling into what looked to be life after baseball in Costa Rica. Later in the season, when Orlando became the darling of the New York media, Alberto Hernández played in Taiwan, still hoping for a chance to get to the United States.

"Four Cuban players and a pitching coach who left for the United States on a flimsy boat a week ago haven't been heard from and their families fear they're lost at sea," the Associated Press reported on March 18. I'd heard the story on National Public Radio earlier that morning and was concerned. The week before, a cold front had moved across the Florida Straits and brought high winds and heavy seas to the Cuban coastline. On the night the front came in, I went to a ball game in Havana wearing a shirt, sweatshirt, and light jacket, and still felt cold in the strong north winds. If the players had embarked on their journey in a small boat a week ago, it was very possible they had drowned. ·

Joe Cubas told reporters he had received a call from worried family members in Cuba who said the men left on March 10. Cubas then contacted Brothers to the Rescue, a Miami-based group that flies over the waters between the United States and Cuba searching for rafters, but there was no sign of the players. The Coast Guard office in Miami, however, said that no one contacted them about the missing players during the entire week.

The most well-known of the group was Jorge Luis Toca, twenty-six at the time he left Cuba, a right-handed-hitting first baseman who had played on *equipo Cuba*. Toca was valued for his strong defensive skills and solid hitting, although he did not possess great power. Like Orlando Hernández, Toca really had no choice but to escape Cuba. He publicly stated he wanted to play in the major leagues—a pronouncement that got him suspended from the Cuban leagues. In 1997, a *Granma* article stated that Toca was banned because he had made it clear he wanted "to leave the country with the idea of being a professional ballplayer."[5] Toca should have played on *equipo Cuba* at the

Atlanta Olympics, but because of his openness he had become a liability. Word in Cuba was that he was even taken off the team plane as it was about to depart for a month of training in Mexico in 1996.

The other players were catcher Angel López, twenty-nine, who had been banned along with Toca and who was indeed a prospect, having been chosen to the preselection for the past two years; Jorge Díaz, twenty-nine, the second baseman for Villa Clara although he had never been on *equipo Cuba* or Cuba B or even taken to the preselection; and a promising younger player, Maykel Jova, age seventeen. The players, all from Villa Clara, were joined by pitching coach Orlando Chinea, forty-one.[6]

I was most interested in Toca. Not only was he a prospect, but I had heard that he had married a Japanese woman, Miyo Yamasaki, while the Cuban team toured there. Some thought his intent was to go back to Japan to play. Certainly the Cuban government did; they had denied him permission to leave the country.

The players had already been missing for over a week, and it seemed there was little hope of finding them alive. At one point, Joe Cubas told the press that the players were in the Dominican Republic at a location he would not disclose. The following day it was announced that the Cubans had been rescued by a fishing boat near Ragged Island in the Bahamas and that they had never been in the Dominican Republic. The source: Joe Cubas. Cubas had, in fact, been the source for almost all of the information about the Toca crew from the start. Cubas said he planned to ask Costa Rica to grant visas to the entire group, which included four other Cubans in addition to the players.[7]

The real story began to emerge. The players were going to leave on March 10, but bad weather and rough seas forced them to put their plans on hold. They traveled, in disguise, to another part of Cuba in a rented car. On March 20, they reportedly sailed from a small town in Las Tunas province in a nineteen-foot boat with a single outboard motor, with no food and only a few containers of water. After seventeen-and-a-half hours at sea, they were rescued by a Bahamian fishing boat.

Shortly after the players arrived at a detention center in Nassau, they began negotiating with Joe Cubas. But other non-baseball-playing Cubans held there were upset that the potential prospects might get special treatment, the same as Orlando Hernández and two other players had received in January.[8] Toca's Japanese wife was his ticket out of the detention center in the Bahamas. Initially, he refused the visa in a show of solidarity with those who had accompanied him on the journey. But within a few days, Toca had changed his mind, accepted the offer, and was off to Japan.[9]

After Toca left, the other three Cuban players and the coach remained in detention in the Bahamas under the threat that they would be deported back to Cuba. Joe Cubas tried to find a third country that would give them asylum but could find none. In the past, he had taken players to the Dominican Republic, but with the election of Leonel Fernández, that option was severed. Cubas then worked through Costa Rica. President José Figueres had earlier helped arrange residency for Rolando Arrojo and Orlando Hernández, but that option was cut off as well. A new president had taken office and, more important, Costa Rica had just experienced a visa-selling scandal involving Cubans, although not baseball players.

The Bahamian government was also feeling pressure. It has an agreement to repatriate Cubans who arrive there illegally, and it saw no reason to give baseball players special treatment. On May 19, sixty-five Cuban refugees, including ballplayers Angel López, Jorge Díaz, and Maykel Jova, and coach Orlando Chinea, were returned to Cuba by the Bahamian government. López, Díaz, Jova, and Chinea had been promised, upon their return to Cuba, visas by officials of the Nicaraguan Embassy in Havana, but the Cuban government had no intention of letting them leave. Cuba's Foreign Ministry declared that if Nicaraguan President Arnoldo Alemán was willing to accept immigrants, he could have all he wanted, but not the three players and the coach, nor any of the other Cubans repatriated from the Bahamas. When President Alemán responded by saying only two visas were necessary, for Fidel Castro and his brother Raúl, it was clear there would be no resolution; the three players and Chinea were stuck in Cuba, where they complained of being constantly watched and even threatened by government authorities.

Cuban baseball commissioner Carlos Rodríguez announced that a scheduled tour of Nicaragua by two Cuban baseball teams had been canceled "because of the unfavorable climate" created by Nicaraguan authorities. "The technical, tactical, psychological, educational and sports objectives of our national teams would not be well served," added Rodríguez.[10]

The "Redefections"

In August, Díaz, López, and Jova, along with two other players, "redefected." Reportedly leaving Cuba by small boat just off the Cuban coast, the group was picked up by a seventy-two-foot yacht chartered by a Fort Lauderdale resident, Nicholas Tanney Nolter, and taken five hundred miles to Puerto Cabezas, Nicaragua. Ninoska Pérez, an official of the Cuban American National Foundation, a Miami-based anti-Castro group, was waiting for them and took the group to Managua where they stayed at the pricey Inter-Continental Hotel. The visas they had been promised in May were also waiting for them, but they could stay only thirty days.

By early 1999, the "redefectors," now in Costa Rica, held a try-out camp for major league scouts. Angel López, age thirty, was trying to pass himself off as twenty-five. Had he been twenty-five, López would have had to begin his career in the Cuban League at age twelve. Nolter, who runs an Internet sports gaming business from San José, Costa Rica, and who has helped others escape from Cuba, now emerged as a broker. He claimed to have had conversations with several major league clubs about the players, who agreed to give him 5 percent of their signing bonuses to offset his expenses. Nolter used the Internet to arrange an agent for the players: Joe Kehoskie, who, before turning to player representation five years earlier, had been the clubhouse manager for the Triple A Rochester Red Wings.

Toca and the Mets

While the "redefectors" were still dreaming of the big leagues from Costa Rica, Jorge Luis Toca surfaced in Los Angeles with agent Don Nomura (who represented New York Yankees pitcher Hideki Irabu). Within a week, Toca signed a contract with the New York Mets and received a signing bonus of between $1.5 and $2 million. The Mets were now aware that he was in fact twenty-seven, not twenty-three as he claimed. They were hoping his long layoff from baseball had not eroded his skills. Toca played in the fall instructional league, the Arizona Fall League, and winter ball in Puerto Rico. In 1999, he made it to the major leagues with the Mets.

The defections of the "El Duque" and Toca groups made it clear that players were beginning to take bigger risks to leave Cuba. As *Sports*

Illustrated reporter S. I. Price summed it up, "What could be more embarrassing for the regime than to have its world-renowned baseball players, the jewel of Cuba's vaunted sports system, risking their lives to get away—or, worse, dying and becoming martyrs?"[11]

While many of the banned players took to the boats, however, one of the best, Germán Mesa, stayed at home.

The Return of Germán Mesa

In the championship baseball game of the 1991 Pan American Games in Havana's Estadio Latinoamericano, sixty thousand fans watched as Cuba led the United States 3–1 in the eighth inning. The bases were loaded with only one out when U.S. catcher Charles Johnson hit the ball between second and third for what seemed like a sure single. But Cuban shortstop, Germán Mesa, dove to his left, caught the ball, and before hitting the ground, threw it to the second baseman who turned an inning-ending double play. No one who saw the game will ever forget it, but for Mesa it was the kind of play he routinely makes.

"I saw Mesa make a play that I did not think was possible. I can still see him in my mind getting to a ball that he should have never been able to reach," recalls Tom Kayser, president of the Texas League, who watched Mesa play in the World Championships in Havana in 1995. "He has incredible body control. If you rated body control on a scale of two to eight, I would give him a ten."

On the two–eight rating scale that is used by Major League Baseball, Mesa was rated in 1990 as five (average) or six (above average) for every aspect of his game except power. Mesa, the regular shortstop for six years on *equipo Cuba*, was the island equivalent of Ozzie Smith. One thing is for sure: he was the best shortstop in Cuba, better than Ordóñez and better than the player who replaced him on *equipo Cuba*, Eduardo Paret.

Mesa, now thirty-one, was in his prime when he was banned for life from Cuba baseball in October 1996 for allegedly taking money from a U.S. player agent. While Orlando Hernández and Alberto Hernández chose to defect, Mesa just disappeared from baseball. He was the Olympic shortstop in 1992 but was left off the 1996 squad, supposedly for *bajo rendimiento* (poor performance), but in truth the Cuban authorities thought Mesa might defect in Atlanta. Mesa was a fan favorite, and they were angry that he was kept from playing. "Banning Germán Mesa is like banning Cal Ripken," said one of the regulars at the *esquina caliente* in Havana's Parque Central. When Mesa's banishment was announced, there were popular protests demanding his reinstatement at the municipal building in his hometown of Cuatro Caminos, near Cotorro, on the outskirts of Havana. As the suspension continued, some fans went to the baseball commissioner's office at the Estadio Latinoamericano petitioning for his return.

No matter where one went in Cuba the talk was about Mesa, about how good he was and how much he was missed. When in Havana in January 1997, I heard there was a possibility of Mesa's reinstatement. "Germán Mesa has been working out," Sigfredo Barros told me. "Mesa said he had no intention of going to stay in the United States. He said 'I talked with a scout and took some money, but I never thought about going to the United States.'" Barros went on to explain that perhaps Mesa should not have been banned for his actions and that he might be allowed to play in the 1997–1998 season. "*Ojalá* [I hope]," said Barros.

He was not. Mesa was relegated to teaching baseball to school kids, which left some Havana fans wondering why, if he was such a bad guy, was he allowed to work with children? But it seemed clear the government was looking for some way to get Mesa back into Cuban baseball without admitting it had made a mistake. Most Cuban fans, knowing the government seldom admitted being wrong, resigned themselves to the fact that they would probably never see Mesa play again. When asked whether they believed Mesa would be allowed back on the field, some fans stroked imaginary beards on their chins—a reference that it was Fidel's call.

Mesa's spirits were crushed by being banned from the game he loved. An additional blow to an already deeply disappointed Mesa was knowing that his understudy, Rey Ordóñez, was enjoying success with the New York Mets. And Ordóñez was earning dollars, something Mesa was prohibited from doing.

It was also tough on the Industriales. They lost Ordóñez in 1993, then Mesa. In a game during the 1997–98 season with a seventeen-year-old rookie at short, I saw second baseman Juan Padilla make a spectacular snag to begin a double play and then freeze and hold on to the ball. A Cuban friend sitting next to me turned and said, "Padilla just remembered that Germán Mesa was not playing shortstop."

Germán Mesa Almost Returns to Cuban Baseball

On January 26, 1998, the day after Pope John Paul II left Cuba, the nightly news program on state-run Cuban television announced that shortstop Germán Mesa; Eduardo Paret, the shortstop on the 1996 Olympic Gold Medal team; outfielder Osmani García; and catcher Angel López—along with two coaches—would all be allowed to return to baseball the following season. The next day Havana was buzzing as fans discussed Mesa's return. Many thought the news was too good to be true. They were right. Two days later the excitement turned into disbelief when *Granma* announced that the reinstatements had not, in fact, occurred and that the sanctions and ban would continue. The bad news was buried in the last paragraph of a game story.

Cuban commissioner Carlos Rodríguez claimed he had been misunderstood by a television reporter. "What the commissioner said was that the players, including Mesa, were training and that the baseball commission was studying their cases," Raúl Arce told me. "EFE, the Spanish news agency, released a cable stating that the issue was resolved. The Cuban TV announcer read the cable and broadcast the information, but it was not official."

"The baseball commissioner did say that Mesa and the others were training and had positive attitudes. He did not say that they were not going to play," Martin Hacthoun, a reporter with the official Cuban news agency Prensa Latina told me. The inference was that the door remained open for the eventual reincorporation of the six into Cuban baseball. There was also speculation that the original announcement was a gesture of goodwill following on the heels of the Pope's visit but that it was rescinded by higher government officials.

Mesa had to be excited to hear the news on television that he had been reinstated. And he must have been devastated to read, only a day later, that it was not true. In any event, it is difficult to imagine that the players and coaches could maintain a "positive attitude" while they continued to be banned from baseball.

Havana, March 1998

When I arrived in Havana in March 1998, I immediately asked about the bizarre events surrounding the reported lifting of Mesa's ban in January. I heard from half a dozen sources that it was "very likely" that Mesa would be allowed to return to play in Cuba. Because the current season was almost over and baseball officials did not want him to return late in the season, his reentry into Cuban baseball would be postponed until the provincial series that runs from May to August—the lowest level of Cuban baseball. Fifteen teams representing divisions within the city of Havana compete on weekends with the best players chosen to move on to one of Havana's two teams in the Serie Nacional. If things went well, Mesa could return to the Industriales in November. I was told again and again that Mesa was working and training in his hometown and that he was maintaining a positive attitude. It began to sound like a mantra.

"Cuban baseball officials have taken into consideration the positive attitude of Germán Mesa, both on and off the field," Barros explained. "He is now in training and it is almost certain he will return to play." Said Arce, "If they are letting him train, it is because he will return, although there has been no official announcement."

Barros and Arce were correct. On March 26, 1998, the commissioner announced that the suspensions against Mesa and the other players had been lifted. Barros noted it in passing in his column on March 27. In May, one of the best shortstops in the world began playing with his local team, Cotorro, at stadiums throughout the Havana area in the intense heat of the Cuban summer.

"If you announced in *Granma* that Germán Mesa will return to play with the Industriales tomorrow, you would fill the entire stadium," said Arce.

8 ☆ The Return of
Rendimiento: The 37th and
38th Series Nacionales

Germán Mesa was nervous as he waited to take the field on opening day of the 1998 baseball season. When he finally ran out to his shortstop position as he had done twelve other seasons, Mesa got on his knees and kissed the infield ground. The forty thousand fans at Estadio Latinoamericano gave him a ten-minute standing ovation while chanting "Ger-mán, "Ger-mán." Mesa could not hold back the tears.

After things quieted down, Mesa motioned for first baseman Antonio Scull to toss him the ball for infield practice. Instead, Scull walked over, handed him the ball, and gave Mesa a huge bear hug. All of Mesa's Industriales teammates, the opposing Pinar del Río players, and the umpires followed suit. Appropriately, the game and the 1998–99 season opened with a roller to short, which Mesa cleanly fielded to throw out the runner at first.

"It was like a Christmas gift," Mesa told me when asked to describe being back in baseball. "It's difficult to explain, but I was able to return to play the game I love. When I heard the fans yelling and I saw all the players coming over to greet me, I was overcome with emotion." It was still hard for Mesa to remain dry-eyed when he recalled the events three months later. What was it like not being allowed to play in the Cuban League for nearly two years? "It was as if someone took away your dream," replied Mesa. "But now I'm back, and that is what is important to me."

I asked a Cuban friend whether Mesa was the first baseball player pardoned. "He is the first Cuban pardoned—period," he responded. While the decision by Fidel to let the country's best shortstop return to the game is unparalleled, and an important symbolic gesture, the more difficult task of improving the quality of Cuban baseball and bringing fans back to the ballparks had begun a year earlier.

After the loss to Japan in 1997, which some in Cuban sports circles refer to as "the disaster in Barcelona," and in the face of the increasing unpopularity of forced player retirement coupled with the ongoing fear of defections, the Cuban baseball program underwent a major overhaul. In the space of three months, the head of INDER, the baseball commissioner, and the manager and general manager of *equipo Cuba* were all replaced.

Although baseball in Cuba in the mid-1990s was in decline, it was by no means in a state of decadence. "The Cuban team, like the Titanic, was unsinkable. But the difference is that the Cuban team can be made to float again," wrote Cuban journalist Carlos Cayetano after the loss in Barcelona.[1]

Carlos Rodríguez, the new baseball commissioner, was the person chosen to right the ship. Rodríguez's official title is Comisionado de Béisbol Cubano (Baseball Commissioner), and he is director of the Comisión Nacional de Béisbol, the group that guides Cuba's most important sport. But he is also beholden to those above him, in INDER, in the Central Committee of the Communist Party—most of whom know little about baseball. Ultimately, he answers to Fidel, who micromanages baseball. Rodríguez works diligently within the limits placed on him from above, and he knew his job would not be easy.

"Being the baseball commissioner in Cuba is like sitting on top of a barrel of gasoline with a fuse in one hand and a match in the other," Rodríguez candidly told me in what otherwise had been a very formal interview in March 1998, in his office under the grandstands at the Estadio Latinoamericano. "You don't want to lose a game."

Rodríguez, from a tobacco-growing family in San Luis in Pinar del Río province, is short, trim, and always seems to have a cigar from his family farm in hand. In his mid-forties, Rodríguez has been working in baseball since 1970. He opened the sports school in Pinar del Río, was sub-director of INDER in the same province and, in the early 1990s, was the first Cuban baseball coach to go to El Salvador.

The cornerstone of Rodríguez's renovation of Cuban baseball is to make advancement to *equipo Cuba* based on *rendimiento* (performance). He wants to make players accountable, not reward past stars who had sub-par seasons. Rodríguez told me that Cuban baseball had not really changed in the past year and that *equipo Cuba* would still be selected by the technical commission. The goal is to select a team "capable of recapturing the victories that Cuban people are accustomed to."

"I insist that we work toward total performance, and not base selection on what a player did in past seasons," explained Rodríguez.[2] Selection to *equipo Cuba* based on *rendimiento histórico* (past performance) was a major criticism of the previous baseball regime in Cuba. "*El terreno tendrá la última palabra* [The playing field will have the final word]," said Rodríguez.

For Rodríguez, selecting the team is not just a matter of picking the player with the best batting average or the pitcher with the most victories.[3] "We hear on TV that *fulano* [so-and-so] is batting .375 and should be on *equipo Cuba*. But look, he only has sixteen RBI and another player is hitting .340 but has forty-five RBI, and in baseball the team that scores the most runs wins." The team would need to have power, skill, speed, pitching depth, and solid defense. Rodríguez explained that the players chosen not only must have good offensive numbers, but must be good defensively. And pitchers would be evaluated not only on wins and loses and ERA, but against which teams they had compiled their records. The commission would also look at the persistence and desire of each player. Does he run out every hit? Does he give his all in every game?

Rodríguez also made it clear that age was not a factor. This was a change from previous teams that had excluded players who would not fit into the next Olympic cycle. "We are not going to stress age; we stress—I repeat—*el rendimiento* [performance]."

The 37th Serie Nacional

The 37th Serie Nacional, which began on November 15, 1997, and ran until the end of April 1998, was Rodríguez's first opportunity to put his ideas into practice. It was only the second time in the past thirty-seven years that the league would play a ninety-game schedule. Normally the Serie Nacional would involve approximately sixty-five games, with the best players then going on to a second season, the Serie Selectiva, with eight teams. One reason for the change was that fans simply did not identify with the teams created for the Serie Selectiva. They wanted to root for their favorite team, and this was especially the case in Havana. For Havana fans, the Industriales were the only team in town. But the players also liked remaining with one team for the entire baseball season.

On my first visit during the 37th Serie Nacional, it appeared that not much had changed from the previous season. The level of play was not substantially better, and the crowds were still small. In December 1997, there were fewer than three hundred people in the fifty-five-thousand-capacity Estadio Latinoamericano for a game between Provincia Habana and the Industriales. All of the fans in attendance that night would have fit comfortably in one of the *camellos* (camels), the huge buses that ply the streets of Havana.

Chico and the Man

Estadio Latinoamericano is the premier baseball park in Cuba. The stadium was inaugurated on October 26, 1946 and expanded to its current capacity in 1971.[4] Ernesto "Chico" Morilla, age seventy-five, has probably seen more baseball games in the stadium than anyone else during the past forty years. Since the early 1960s, he has worked at Estadio Latinoamericano, standing at the entrance to the box seats just behind home plate and making sure Cuban sports officials, visiting press, and former players are accommodated. Chico is a delightful person, and visiting with him was always one of the highlights of my visits to the stadium.

Chico pitched for Cienfuegos and Habana in the Cuban professional league, and with Miami Beach in the Florida International League (the same league in which the Havana Cubans participated). In 1946 at Miami Beach, he was 23–9 with a 2.03 ERA and six shutouts. He also played for the Houston Buffs in 1949, and he enjoys reminiscing about the high caliber of play in the Double A Texas League.

"I remember this guy Gray who only had one arm," said Morilla, referring to Pete Gray, who played with the St. Louis Browns in 1945 but was with the Dallas team in 1949. "He could really hit the ball a long way, but he couldn't hit a change-up, so that's what I threw him." But the strikeout Morilla will never forget was when he faced Stan Musial.

"Because we were a St. Louis Cardinals farm club, the major league team would play an exhibition game in Houston every year. Musial fouled off the first two pitches, and I thought to myself, 'What do I throw this guy?' I decided I would go with a fastball down the middle."

"Strike three," said Morilla, raising his arm to indicate the umpire's call. Recalls Chico, "If Musial would have hit that pitch, it would have gone 500 feet. He turned and looked at me and said, 'You son of a bitch.'" But Musial was not really angry, and he gave Chico a small memento. The next day Chico brought to the stadium and proudly showed me a small plastic statue of Stan the Man given to him by Musial in Houston fifty years earlier. It was the highlight of his career.

When I returned to the Estadio Latinoamericano in March 1998 for a game between Provincia Habana and the Industriales, the same two teams I had seen only three months earlier, there were about twenty-five thousand loud fans very much into the game.

"The last time there was a crowd this exciting was the fifth game of the play-offs in 1995, Orlando Hernández against Rolando Arrojo," said Barros, and then grasping the implication of that statement—that the last time the crowd was this good was with two pitchers who had since defected, recovered and said, "The fans are now learning the new players. The all-star game helped, and baseball is picking up again."

The 1998 All-Star Game

I had arranged to go on a road trip with the team from Pinar del Río, although not for the entire twenty-two-day road trip. Pinar del Río left on February 16 for a three-game series in Guantánamo, a seventeen- to eighteen-hour bus ride, followed by series in Santiago de Cuba, Camagüey, Las Tunas, Matanzas, and Isla de la Juventud, before returning home on March 10. My plan was to catch up with the team in Nueva Gerona, the capital of Isla de la Juventud, for a weekend series.

A couple of weeks before the trip, I received word that the entire baseball schedule had been canceled for the weekend of March 7–8 because of the all-star game in Ciego de Ávila. I had never heard of an all-star game in Cuba, but Cuban journalists insisted that there had been such games in the past but that they had been played only at the end of the year. An all-star game after seventy games of a ninety-game schedule was clearly an afterthought.

Told by baseball officials that I could attend the game, my next challenge was getting to Ciego de Ávila, a city in the geographic center of Cuba. I could ride the bus with the baseball officials or with the Cuban press corps, or fly on Cubana Air Lines. Because the buses were to leave before my arrival in Havana, I had to fly. "Ciego," as it is known in Cuba, has a modern new airport, but most flights arrive directly from Toronto or Montreal with Canadian tourists headed for the beach resorts at Cayo Coco, about thirty miles to the north.

The all-star game weekend was really a preview of the players who would be in the mix for *equipo Cuba*, and a wake-up call for some players who were not invited. In fact, about half of the twenty-two players on the 1997 *equipo Cuba* were not selected for the all-star rosters. Among the absentees was Omar Linares. He had not played in nearly a month due to a knee injury, but some in baseball thought he was not making the extra effort and that part of the reason his knee hurt was that it had about ten extra pounds to support.

Another player not invited was power pitcher Pedro Luis Lazo, who was having a mediocre year. Lazo was sent a handwritten note from someone in the baseball commission office saying that his absence from the all-star game was to put him on notice; he had better put out more effort during the last few weeks of the season or he would not be chosen to the preselection training camp in May.

Las Estrellas bajo las Estrellas

Much like the hoopla that surrounds the Major League All-Star Game each summer, the entire weekend was programmed to be a reward for the players and a celebration of Cuban baseball. On Saturday morning, the players and Cuban press corps went to the beach at Cayo Coco, and in the evening the two teams went to block parties organized by Comités de Defensa de la Revolución (Committees for the Defense of the Revolution)—CDRs—the neighborhood organizations formed in 1960 to defend the government against internal opposition, but that are also used to conduct immunization campaigns or to arrange celebrations for special events.

The open-air block parties, billed as *las estrellas bajo las estrellas* (the stars under the stars), exemplified how much a part of the Cuban people these players are. For a couple of hours, Cuba's best baseball players mingled with thousands of fans (not one asked for an autograph), visited with people in their living rooms and kitchens, and took part in skits with local comedians. Antonio Pacheco, two-time Olympic second baseman on *equipo Cuba*, went up on an improvised stage in someone's front yard and was treated like the guy next door while being made the butt of good-natured jokes.

It was clear the players are close to the fans and are always accessible. It is not unusual to see Pinar del Río pitcher Pedro Luis Lazo walking down the street after a home game in his uniform pants and T-shirt, eating an ice cream cone, or *equipo Cuba* pitcher José Ibar in his uniform chatting with his neighbors just outside the stadium before a ball game in San José de las Lajas.

Ciego de Ávila is a provincial capital of eighty-five thousand inhabitants. Horse-drawn wagons dominate the roadways, occasionally making way for the most common means of public transportation, the bici-taxi, which consists of a wooden platform on a frame pulled by a bicycle. The all-star game was awarded to Ciego de Ávila because its baseball team had a great year and the die-hard fans fill the stadium win or lose.

On all-star Sunday, the crowd assembled early. The gates opened around 8:00 A.M. (admission was one peso—five cents), although the pregame ceremonies would not begin until 1:30 and the start of the game itself was almost eight hours away. The price was also one peso to park a bicycle in an enclosed lot, which was full. Estadio José Ramón Cepero was named for a young revolutionary from Ciego de Ávila. The stadium holds about ten thousand in the covered grandstands, and another five thousand standing outside the fence along the first baseline, sitting on top of outfield fences, or sitting on trucks parked near the fence. At 9:30 A.M. when I arrived, "Home Club" was being painted in English over a dugout and the stands were about 80 percent full; at 10:00 A.M., no seats were available. Most fans stayed until 7:00 P.M., when the game ended.

The all-star game was obviously more than a game—it was an attempt by government officials to draw on the deep roots of baseball in Cuba. If I had been given an inside look at baseball on the island on previous trips, I was now being taken to the heart of Cuban baseball.

Shortly before the opening ceremony, a two-year-old strolled out to home plate with a full-size bat and began to take swings in the air! Then he went to a special mound—about twenty-five feet from home—and with an adult glove on his hand, glared in at the catcher, shook off a sign, and threw the ball over the plate. The crowd roared. At 1:35 P.M., with people throughout Cuba watching on national television, about twenty children came onto the field, some dressed as gymnasts, others as weight lifters, and two four-year-olds as boxers. After marching around for a few minutes, they exited and two hundred doves were released from the pitcher's mound.

This display was followed by the introduction of some veteran players, now retired from the game but still fan favorites, including Luis Casanova, Lourdes Gourriel, Antonio Muñoz, and Wilfredo Sánchez. The skills contests (*espectáculos de habilidades*) that followed included a home run–hitting match won by Orestes Kindelán, who hit four monster blasts. Another contest involved a player hitting a ball and then running to first. Outfielder Roger Poll was the fastest. Another competition had an outfielder throwing the ball from center field to home, and Roger Poll had a toss land six inches from the plate.

The final event before the all-star game featured the two teams that played for the national championship in the nine- to ten-year-old division, Villa Clara and runner-up Ciego de Ávila, in a three-inning contest. After the game ended, the young players lined up around the edge of the infield grass. The Cuban all-star players walked on the field and each carried one young player off the field in his arms. It was emotional and very impressive, and it clearly illustrated the depth of the meaning of baseball to Cuba. It truly was the passing of the game to the next generation.

Just before game time, a delegation from the Japanese amateur baseball federation—including twelve managers—came in and was seated behind home plate. Seeing the Japanese at a very important ceremonial event in Cuban baseball illustrated the extent to which U.S. baseball is being left out. The Japanese come two or three times a year to discuss baseball agreements with the Cubans. Many of the Cuban baseball coaches, trainers, and players approached the Japanese contingent and warmly greeted the group—bowing and speaking in Japanese.

Commissioner Rodríguez introduced me to Eiichiro Yamamoto, the head of the Japanese amateur baseball federation. "Yami," now in his eighties, has been to Cuba over one hundred times since his first visit in 1971. There is a plaque signed by Yamamoto under the grandstands in Estadio Latinoamericano in Japanese and Spanish, which commemorates the fiftieth anniversary of the park. Yami's visits have resulted in Cuban players and coaches going to Japan for extended periods of time and working with both Industrial League teams and clubs from Japanese professional baseball. *Equipo Cuba* is a frequent visitor to Japan; first baseman Orestes Kindelán told me he had been to Tokyo more than a dozen times.

After the game I had to rush to meet the Cuban press corps for the long bus ride back to Havana. They were staying at the Motel del Partido—the Party Motel, the Communist Party. This was a place for rest and relaxation, a reward for those who played by the rules of the system. I dozed off on the bus shortly after we left Ciego de Ávila at 10:00 P.M. and woke up to see the shadows of the Sierra del Escambray. A few hours later in the middle of nowhere, the bus came to a sudden stop. No one complained, and the driver matter-of-factly reached for an extra fan belt and made the repair. Upon arriving in Havana, the twenty-five members of the media were delivered to their homes. I was one of the last, finally reaching my apartment at 5:00 A.M. It was quite a trip—one, I learned later, that had earned me the respect of Cuban journalists who knew I had the option of flying back.

Road Trip to Pinar del Río

I travelled to Pinar del Río, about one hundred miles west of Havana, for the first game after the all-star break. Estadio Capitán San Luis, named for a hero of the Revolution, is a beautiful park with covered grandstands from foul pole to foul pole and a capacity of about twenty thousand. As in all Cuban ballparks, there were no paid advertisements, just political slogans.

While his teammates were already working out in their game uniforms, Omar Linares appeared in his sweats. We greeted each other, and he went off to stretch. Even at thirty, he still has the face of *El Niño* (the kid). After his workout, he went home, put on his uniform, and came back to play—his first action in almost a month. Pinar del Río would need his bat during the play-offs set to begin in a few weeks.

The starter for Pinar del Río in the evening's game against the Metropolitanos was Pedro Luis Lazo, whom I had never seen pitch. I sat in the first row behind the home dugout and could clearly see from only a few feet away the determined expression on Lazo's face as he came in from the mound after each inning. The 6'5", 225-lb., right-handed power pitcher was on fire. Lazo must have taken the message from the baseball commission to heart.

While his fastball has been clocked at ninety-eight miles an hour, he has good movement on the ball and has developed great control—something he was lacking only a couple of years back. After each of Lazo's strikeouts, the crowd of twelve thousand would count off the strikeouts, "Uno, dos, tres . . ." The fans were hoarse because Lazo had fanned sixteen opposing batters by game's end. And while Lazo maintained his intensity, he was relaxed, even stopping to talk to kids in the stands before going out for the ninth inning. He won the game 4–1, giving up only two hits. My notes read "Lazo may be the best pitcher in Cuba. This kid could walk in and start in major leagues right now." But he was Pinar del Río's second starter; José Ariel Contreras was considered better.

The outstanding play of the regular season extended into the play-offs. José Ibar, who became Cuba's first twenty-game winner during the season, guided his Provincia Habana team over Pinar del Río, and Lazo, 2–1 with both pitchers going the distance. Four days later, Ibar beat Lazo again by a 2–1 margin, this time in ten innings and again with both players pitching complete games. But Pinar del Río won the series, and went on to beat Santiago in the finals.

New players emerged during the season. Loidel Chapellí (Camagüey) established himself as the country's top first baseman. Roberquis Videaux (Guantánamo), a left-handed-hitting outfielder, led the league in hitting with a .393 average, and Roger Poll (Ciego de Ávila) also had an outstanding season. Outfielder Yasser Gómez (the Metropolitanos) set the record for hits by a rookie with 112, finished fifth in the league in hitting with a .359 average, and was selected as Rookie of the Year. Because he was only eighteen, he played for the Cuban junior team instead of *equipo Cuba*.

Then there was the solid performace of a young pitcher from the Industriales, Adrián Hernández, who ended the year with a 10–6 record. Although he is no relation to Orlando "El Duque" Hernández, Adrián wears his socks in the style of "El Duque," has a similar build to the Yankee pitcher, and has a similar windup. And like "El Duque," he is a great fielder. Fans refer to him as "a shortstop in the box." He does not like it when the fans in Havana shout "El Duque" while he's on the mound, but the similarity between the two Hernándezes was such that Adrián was referred to by members of the Peña at the Parque Central as *el duque de cartón* (imitation duke).

Cuban baseball seemed to be revitalized. If the all-star game was the symbolic affirmation of Cuban baseball, it was the concrete efforts of Rodríguez and the baseball commission that had reinvigorated the game on the field. And the efforts to upgrade Cuban baseball included plans to send coaches to remote areas and develop the strong roots of the game even further. Clearly the fans had returned. During the playoffs in Havana, crowds of forty thousand plus were common, and in the provinces, the parks were also packed.

The End of Retirement

Near the end of the regular season, Commissioner Rodríguez announced that the program of allowing players to retire and play abroad had been curtailed. Eleven players, including Víctor Mesa, would go to Japan, but they would be the last group. Further, Rodríguez noted, bans had been lifted against Germán Mesa, Eduardo Paret, Osmani García, and two coaches because of their good behavior and positive attitudes.

The decision to change the policy on retirement clearly came from high in the Cuban government. It was rumored that Fidel was upset that baseball players needed economic incentives to represent their country abroad. Admitting that not even baseball players could be swayed by moral incentives would be a clear indication that his revolution had indeed failed. And on a more practical note, Fidel thought earning a little money only tempted players to think about earning more by defecting.

While the 37th Serie Nacional was indeed a revival of Cuban baseball, the government was quick to declare it a complete victory for the Revolution. For Fidel, it was an example of *el triunfo de la pelota libre sobre la pelota esclava* (the victory of free baseball over slave baseball). While some true believers attribute the rebirth of Cuban baseball to increased revolutionary fever, clearly the policy of *rendimiento* was in great part responsible for the improved level of play in the Serie Nacional. *Rendimiento* was not the only policy change however. Almost everyone I spoke with during 1997 and 1998 believed players needed more incentives: if a player could just have enough dollars to meet his family's necessities, he would be less likely to defect.

The issue of incentives had been discussed by baseball officials during the crisis. These incentives could include cash bonuses and prizes.[5] By early 1999, conversations with members of the Cuban media revealed that, in fact, an incentives policy had been introduced, although I don't believe it was ever officially announced. One method was to give players representing Cuba in international competitions a per diem in dollars, while still covering all of their expenses. Thus, in 1998, a player on *equipo Cuba* who trained in Mexico and played in tournaments in Holland, Italy, and Venezuela might be able to accumulate as much as $1,500. Players also were given access to a dollar store in the Estadio Latinoamericano where they would receive a 20-percent discount on products. I was also told that baseball officials would often help players on an ad hoc basis, *resolver* their *necesidades*. This could be in the form of helping locate more adequate housing or obtaining a new set of tires for their cars, for example. I even heard that Javier Méndez was given a car on his birthday by Fidel.

These new incentives are not institutionalized but are parceled out in a paternalistic manner. Rather than making the players privileged, the incentives let some of them achieve only a status that many Cubans with dollars already have. More important, they do not apply to all four hundred players who participate in the Serie Nacional, but only to those selected to the elite squads that travel abroad.

1998 *Equipo Cuba*

From the statements made by baseball commissioner Rodríguez, it was obvious that *rendimiento* was going to be the most important factor in the selection of *equipo Cuba*. The meeting at the end of April to select the national team included all sixteen managers—something that had never occurred before—fourteen provincial sports officials, the members of the baseball commission, and selected members of the press corps. Commissioner Rodríguez explained that in addition to *rendimiento*, selection would be based upon other factors—including power, good defense, a balance between left- and right-handed pitchers, and a combination of youth and experience. Also factored were intangibles such as discipline and patriotism.

One member of the Cuban media told me he had expected a rather difficult meeting involving disagreements over player selection and was relieved his fears were not met. He described the event as "very democratic in which everyone had a voice and a vote."

In a departure from past procedures, there was no preselection in 1998. Instead, two teams of twenty-two players each were selected. The average age of players for the 1998 *equipo Cuba* was 27.9, as compared with the 29.8 average of the team that represented Cuba in Atlanta in 1996. Only seven members of the Atlanta group were on the team. Only nine played on the team that lost in the Intercontinental Cup in Barcelona in 1997. This represented a 59-percent change in the team in one year.

The team easily won the World Championships in Italy and Central America and the Caribbean Games in Venezuela during the summer. They won seventeen consecutive games, and *equipo Cuba* was back on track.

38th Serie Nacional

Although the 37th Serie Nacional was indeed a rebirth of Cuban baseball, some wondered whether it was an aberration or whether the changes put in place would result in quality baseball and full stadiums during the next season. From Germán Mesa's emotional return on opening day through the play-offs, the 38th Serie Nacional was, according to most observers, equal to or better than the 37th. The excitement ranged from three consecutive triples in one game by Yasser Gómez, to an unassisted triple play by Villa Clara third baseman Orlando Acebey. With the bases loaded, Acebey picked a grounder from the Industriales Juan Padilla, stepped on third, tagged the runner advancing toward the plate, and then proceeded to tag Padilla, who was a few feet from home, arguing that the ball was hit off his foot.

Pinar del Río second baseman Yobal Dueñas continued to impress with his bat and finished with a league-leading .418 average. And two new stars emerged: Michel Enríquez, a twenty-year-old third baseman from Isla de la Juventud, who broke the all-time hit record held by Wilfredo "El hombre hit" Sánchez (included in his 152 hits in ninety games were a record-breaking thirty-five doubles); and nineteen-year-old Maels Rodríguez, a right-hander from Sancti Spíritus, who displayed a ninety-seven-mile-an-hour fastball with a tremendous curve and a slider.

In an effort to make the Industriales even better, Rookie of the Year Yasser Gómez was traded from the Metropolitanos. When I mentioned to several fans that it seemed the Industriales got the better of the deal, their response was, "Sure, but most fans want to see the Industriales and if they have a better team, more people will go to the stadium."

Throughout Cuba, the fans filled the stadiums because the general level of baseball was high, players were no longer retiring, and the Industriales were winning. There were still frequent blackouts in provincial stadiums, and transporting the teams across the island was still problematic. But Cuban baseball, moribund only two years earlier, was enjoying its second consecutive successful season.

Due to the rapid increase in robberies and street assaults, I no longer walked to the stadium but instead hired a driver to shuttle me between the park and the hotel. In early January 1999, the Cuban government, alarmed by the increase in crime and in an effort to reassert control, placed a policeman at almost every corner. Cubans were routinely stopped and asked to show their identification. By March, the police presence was now firmly established, and the resentment of their constant intrusion into everyday life was palpable.

The Industriales reached the play-offs, dispatched Provincia Habana in three games, and defeated Isla de la Juventud in a series that went seven games, including the final game before sixty thousand fans at Estadio Latinoamericano. The Industriales would face Santiago de Cuba in the finals, and the first two games would be in Havana. I would finally get to see what Gilberto Dihigo described as the ultimate battle in Cuban baseball.

At game one, there were more than fifty thousand fans, most of whom were in their seats an hour before the first pitch. The atmosphere was totally different from any game I had ever experienced in Cuba. Not only were there more people, but the people were louder, and the sound of air horns, drums, and timbals was nonstop. There was, for the first time in more than twenty years, the sound of a ball coming off a wooden bat. In preparation for the new international rules, the Cubans used wooden bats in the play-offs. During the game, Germán Mesa made two incredible plays, unleashing an eruption of excitement from the vast majority which was rooting for the hometown Industriales.

But it was a non-baseball event that provided the most memorable moment of the evening. In the seventh inning, about twenty uniformed police entered along the right-field wall and took positions against the wall in fair territory. These were the new and ever-present police, dressed in dark gray pants, light gray shirts, and black berets. I was told there had been a problem at the stadium earlier in the week when jubilant fans poured onto the field, breaking down the right-field wall while celebrating the Industriales' victory over Isla de la Juventud.

When the police first appeared, the crowd began to whistle in disapproval. The whistling increased in volume and began to reverberate through the stadium. Fans began to yell *"Palestino, Palestino, Palestino,"* ending the refrain with *"Pa'lla,"* a Cuban expression meaning "out of here." *Palestino* (Palestinian) is the Havana term for a person from eastern Cuba, or more generally, for anyone from outside of Havana. The term also connotes someone who is landless or a refugee, and more important, it is the term most frequently used to describe the police, the majority of whom are from eastern Cuba. What occurred at the Estadio Latinoamericano was a public outcry against the increased police presence that had been building during the previous three months. The police were finally ordered off the field by an umpire, and the game resumed. A friend told me he could hear the chanting at his house five blocks from the stadium. And the entire episode was seen on national television throughout Cuba.

The Industriales won the game 3–2 and then defeated Santiago de Cuba the next night in a dramatic comeback 8–7, to take a two-game lead in the best-of-seven series. The series then shifted to Santiago de Cuba for the next three games. The Industriales won the first and appeared ready to capture the championship, but Santiago won four consecutive games, including the last two in Havana to capture the title. Orestes Kindelán had two home runs in the seventh game. It was a dramatic end to an exciting season, and it squashed any discussion that the 37th Serie Nacional had been an aberration.

San José de las Lajas

San José de las Lajas is a small industrial town about twenty miles from downtown Havana and is the home field for the team from Provincia Habana. For several years, San José was the site of the national baseball training center, and it is still occasionally used to train *equipo Cuba*.

After negotiating his way out of the city, my driver entered the *ocho vías*—the limited access road that extends several hundred miles from Pinar del Río toward Santiago de Cuba. As the name implies, the road has eight lanes, which are seldom marked. With almost no traffic, for long stretches the freeway looks more like an airport runway than a highway.

As we turned off the *ocho vías*, the light towers from the stadium in San José were soon visible, and within minutes we entered the Complejo Deportivo Nelson Fernández. The complex includes a very large covered basketball court, a running track and, of course, a baseball stadium. As I walked through the stadium, I was intrigued by a large portrait of Nelson Fernández under the grandstands. Fernández, from the San José area, was not yet fifteen when he died in April 1961 at Playa Girón (the Bay of Pigs). Estadio Nelson Fernández, a very nice small ballpark with an immaculately manicured infield, has a capacity of three thousand. For important games, fans line the open chain-link fences along the baselines.

Commissioner Rodríguez arranged for Nelson Ciero to show me around San José de las Lajas. Ciero, in his mid-fifties and a member of the national technical commission for baseball, graciously answered each question in depth. Ciero's job is to ensure that all works smoothly at the ballparks utilized in the Serie Nacional throughout Cuba. He spends a couple of weeks in each city, checking on the motels that will house the players and on the food they'll be served. He also supervises stadium operations and sees that the proper baseball instruction is being provided.

As we stood outside the stadium at sunset, I asked Ciero about José Ibar, who plays with the Provincia Habana team and, as if on cue, Ibar appeared in the distance. "Here comes Ibar now. People around here call him Cheo," said Ciero.

Ibar, in his game uniform and wearing a warm-up jacket, had been walking on the running track talking to a couple of friends. Ibar, twenty-nine, is very self-confident and congenial. Although he was born in Santiago, his family moved to San José when he was eleven.

Ibar is a veteran of twelve seasons. He had been selected for *equipo Cuba* as early as 1990 but was shelved in the mid-1990s due to an injury. During the 1997–98 season, Ibar went 20–2 in ninety games, becoming the only twenty-game winner in the thirty-seven years of current amateur baseball. He also had a league-leading 1.51 ERA and, to complete the triple crown, led the league in strikeouts with 189 in 196.1 innings. He won four more games in the play-offs, compiling a record 24–2 in 102 games. He was 18–2 in the 1998–1999 season.

We three discussed Ibar's pitching. Ibar's fastball is only in the low nineties, and he does not have a curve. "I throw a slider, split finger, and I try to mix my pitches and change speeds," said Ibar. I had seen Ibar pitch last against the Industriales in the Estadio Latinoamericano before twenty-five thousand fans. He threw inside to a batter and on the next pitch, hit him. "You have to throw inside or you give away too much of the plate," he said. I reminded him that on the first inside pitch the crowd chanted in unison "*Descarado, descarado*" (shameless). "And then when I hit him on the next pitch they all yelled '*Hijo de puta*,'" Ibar laughed.

Nelson Ciero was signed by Alex Pompez (the same scout who allegedly offered Fidel a contract) to the San Francisco Giants in 1959 when he was only fourteen (he was told to lie about his age) and went to the United States to play professional baseball. His last professional contract was with the El Paso team in the Class D Sophomore League in 1961. When his career ended, he was just sixteen years old. Ciero returned to Cuba in April 1961 and began to work as a coach in the new *béisbol revolucionario*. He is now in his thirty-eighth year, although he spent three years in Japan, including one as a coach with the Yokohama team in the Central League. He has a university degree in physical culture and is working on a master's degree in baseball, a new program initiated in Cuba in 1998.

While events were unfolding at Playa Girón in April 1961, Ciero was in El Paso. Given the choice of returning to Cuba or staying in the United States, he went home, realizing he might never have that opportunity again. I was struck by the irony of the two teenage boys named Nelson. Nelson Fernández was killed at Playa Girón and had a stadium named after him. Nelson Ciero came home because of Playa Girón and has devoted his life to baseball.

Two other players, Tito Fuentes and Bert Campaneris, on tour with a Cuban team in Costa Rica during the invasion at Playa Girón, decided not to go home and instead pursued major league careers. Soon after Playa Girón, the United States began its embargo of Cuba, which would come to define relations between the two countries for the next four decades.

"If baseball ever ends, and you see a dead Cuban by the side of the road, you will know it is me," said Ciero. "I can't do anything but this."

9 ☆ "Bring on the Gold Rush": Major League Baseball and Cuba

In the 1950s, one scout—Joe Cambria—and one team—the Washington Senators—focused on one country—Cuba. There were so many Cubans playing for the Senators that, on July 23, 1960, the team was able to record the big leagues' only all-Cuban triple play. In the third inning with no one out and runners at first and second, Kansas City outfielder Whitey Herzog hit a line drive to pitcher Pedro Ramos, who tossed the ball to first baseman Julio Becquer, who relayed the throw to shortstop José Valdivielso covering at second.[1]

"I was the first to hit into an all-Cuban triple play," Herzog told me when I asked him about the event almost thirty years later, adding, "and the last." But maybe not. Although Cuba has been off-limits to Major League Baseball for almost forty years, all organizations look forward to the prospect of again having access to the island's players.

Cuba was a major supplier of players to U.S. professional baseball prior to 1959. Although a few players, such as Tony Oliva, Tony Pérez, Luis Tiant, Jr., and Cookie Rojas, were in the minor league pipeline and made their major league debuts after Fidel came to power, and although Bert Campaneris and Tito Fuentes left in 1962, for the past forty years Cuban baseball talent generally has remained on the island.

Fred Claire, who until 1998 was the general manager and executive vice president of the Los Angeles Dodgers, the leading team in signing Latin American players, believes Cuba will be a major source of players for U.S. baseball. "If the talent was available in Cuba, and

119

all clubs could go in and scout, and sign or draft, I can only envision a gold rush."

To get an idea of how much talent there is in Cuba, one need only look at Puerto Rico and the Dominican Republic. If Puerto Rico, with only one-third of Cuba's population, had only amateur ball, Juan González, Bernie Williams, Sandy and Roberto Alomar, Edgar Martínez, Iván Rodríguez, and Carlos Baerga would not be playing in the major leagues. The Dominican Republic, with three million fewer residents than Cuba, has fifteen hundred players signed to U.S. professional baseball contracts. How many players would Cuba, with a much more highly developed baseball system, produce? One U.S. scout told me he thought each U.S. organization could sign at least twenty Cuban players—from young prospects through major league talent.

Although the U.S. baseball commissioner's office has a ban on talking with Cuban players, this doesn't keep scouts from pulling out their radar guns and stopwatches whenever they have an opportunity to see Cuban teams in international competition. Cuba's junior team, composed of seventeen- and eighteen-year-olds, also has players abroad in international competitions, and major league scouts are always in attendance. There were sixty scouts at a tournament in Monterrey, Mexico, in 1992, where seventeen-year-old Liván Hernández threw a no-hitter.

But the only players fans in the United States know anything about are the defectors—principally Liván and Orlando Hernández, Rolando Arrojo, and Rey Ordóñez—and a very small core of the stars of Cuban baseball, the players who have been the backbone of *equipo Cuba* for the past decade—Omar Linares, Orestes Kindelán, Antonio Pacheco, and Germán Mesa.

Major League Baseball is more interested in the young Cuban players who are unknown in the United States. More than eight hundred players participate in the Serie Nacional and Serie de Desarrollo, and U.S. teams have scouting reports on only a handful of them. Virtually nothing is known about Cuban players between the ages of fifteen and eighteen, the prime ages for signing professional contracts.

What sets the Cuban players apart from other players coming out of Latin America? "Physically, they are faster and they have tremendous reflexes. Mentally, they are very quick, and they have an intuition to play baseball," says Andrés Reiner, assistant to the general manager of the Houston Astros, and the scout who established the Astros' highly-successful Venezuelan baseball academy. Reiner, who has had the opportunity to watch Cuban players for the past decade, is also impressed with the educational level of the Cuban players and the fact that they come from a disciplined system. He believes this would give them an advantage in making the difficult adjustment to playing in the United States.

But like Cuban cigars in the United States, the few Cuban players who have defected have often been overpriced. Why are Cuban players so overvalued? Because they are exotic, writes columnist Tracy Ringolsby: "Put the word Cuban in front a player's name, and the teams are ready to add zeroes behind the dollar sign on their contracts."[2]

Most scouts agree it is difficult to get an accurate reading on just how good Cuban players are because they use aluminum bats, face poor competition, and lack state-of-the-art instruction. But they know the raw talent is there. "Who does Cuba face in its international competitions? The U.S. team is mainly composed of university students with little international experience," said René Arocha. "On the other hand, the Cuban team has played together for a long time and has players who would have been in the big leagues."

"Cuban baseball needs to go to the next level. It is better than you see played on the field at international competitions," *Deportivamente* producer Pedro Cruz González told me, echoing a sentiment heard throughout the island. "When you realize that you are going to win, you don't play as hard."

One Cuban fan complained that baseball on the island was *estancado* (stagnant). While he thought Germán Mesa was a better shortstop than Rey Ordóñez, he felt Ordóñez's three years of experience in the major leagues had allowed him to bypass Mesa. Tito, an elderly member of the Peña, explained it in a more colorful manner. "Germán Mesa has finished at a very good prep school," said Tito, "while Rey Ordóñez has already completed his university degree."

"In 2000, we will have a good team. I believe our team could stay in the game with anybody," said Miguel Valdés. "The Olympics are a short event, and we are specialists at playing short events. But playing against major leaguers is something we have never had to do." The ultimate test would be to play against a U.S. major league team, and that had never happened until the Baltimore Orioles visited Havana in March 1999. But efforts to have a big league team visit Cuba began as early as 1960.

Torrential rains in Florida in March 1959 forced the cancellation of so many spring training games that Cincinnati Reds general manager Gabe Paul called Bobby Maduro, president of the Cuban Sugar Kings of the Triple A International League, to ask whether he could take his Cincinnati team to Cuba for the weekend. Maduro was thrilled, and with only one day's notice, arranged a three-game series in Havana at the Gran Stadium, now the Estadio Latinoamericano, between Cincinnati and the Los Angeles Dodgers. Rain delayed the Reds' arrival, and eventually only two games were played.

In the first game, Don Drysdale pitched seven innings and "cha-cha-chaed through the ranks of the Reds with virtual disdain," reported the *Los Angeles Times*.[3] The Dodgers won 3–2. The next day, Sandy Koufax pitched five innings, and Carl Erskine got the victory in the Dodgers' 4–3 win.

Havana fans were delighted to see Duke Snider, Jim Gilliam, and John Roseboro. And the *Times*'s game story featured gems such as "several score of pistol packin' rebels were in the stadium today." The games were played less than three months after Fidel Castro had ousted Batista.

Since the Reds and Dodgers left Havana on March 21, 1959, no U.S. teams had played on the island, notwithstanding numerous efforts to send major league teams to Cuba, until the Orioles' visit in 1999. "I believe it was 1960 when Baltimore was going to play Cincinnati here in Havana," recalled Marcelo Sánchez in early 1999. "It was called off because the proceeds from the game were going to be used for the agrarian reform movement in Cuba and there was some disagreement over that." Marcelo promised to check on the details, and within a few weeks had sent a packet of newspaper clips on the Baltimore-Cincinnati series that did not happen.

In November 1959, it was announced that the two teams would play a three-game series in Havana beginning March 28, 1960. Baltimore general manager Lee MacPhail canceled the games at the last minute, stating that some of the Baltimore players refused to participate due to the unsafe conditions in the country.[4] Bobby Maduro fired off a telegram to Cincinnati general manager Gabe Paul thanking him for his efforts, and another to MacPhail castigating him for calling off the games and thus spoiling the opportunity to help alleviate the tension between the two countries. It was not the last time Maduro would be upset by U.S. professional baseball during the year.

In July 1960, Maduro's Cuban Sugar Kings franchise was relocated to Jersey City, New Jersey. U.S. Secretary of State Christian Herter asked Commissioner of Baseball Ford Frick to take the step, ostensibly to protect U.S. players from possible anti-American aggression in Cuba. The decision was made only a few days after President Eisenhower eliminated the sugar quota (the above-market price paid for Cuban sugar) and the Cubans began taking steps to nationalize U.S. sugar holdings on the island.[5] It is indeed ironic that the United States took the Sugar Kings from Cuba at the same time that Cuba took back sugar production on the island.

Later in 1960, Herter pressured Frick to prohibit U.S. players from competing in the Cuban winter league. In 1960–61, Habana, Almendares, Marianao, and Cienfuegos played with only Cuban players for the first time since 1905. It was the last professional season in Cuba.

There were no attempts by U.S. professional teams to go to Cuba during the rest of the 1960s as conflict between the two countries deepened. In 1971, Preston Gómez, then manager of the San Diego Padres, announced plans to take a major league all-star team, including Cubans Tony Pérez, Tony Taylor, Tony Oliva, and Leo Cárdenas, to Havana. The tour would have "good will value for the United States similar to the recent table tennis team's trip to Red China," said Gómez.[6] While Gómez received the approval of Commissioner Bowie Kuhn, he was denied permission by the U.S. government.

Pedro Gómez was born on a sugar plantation—Central Preston—in eastern Cuba and, because everybody called him Preston, officially adopted that name when he became a U.S. citizen. Gómez was signed by Joe Cambria and, in 1944, played eight games for the Washington Senators. He later managed the Padres, the Houston Astros, and the Chicago Cubs. He has made regular visits to Cuba for the past four decades and, in 1999, supplied the Cubans with dozens of wooden bats as they prepared both for the new changes in international baseball and to face professional teams.

In early 1975, Gómez met with Cuban baseball officials who expressed interest in having a U.S. professional team play a series in Cuba that March. The U.S. government was also very interested, and a State Department official noted that "U.S. major league baseball has a magic value in projecting a positive image of the U.S. wherever the sport is played."[7]

Commissioner Kuhn met with Cuban baseball officials in Mexico City in February. In addition to the series in question, Kuhn got the impression that "the Cubans are thinking about their relationship with U.S. professional baseball. They have done their best to develop their talents, but being shut out of professional ball here hurts. They would now like Cuban players to be able to look forward to the opportunity to play some day in our major leagues."[8]

Secretary of State Henry Kissinger made it clear that he opposed a U.S. team going to Cuba but nevertheless asked the State Department to send their arguments as to why it should happen. "The Chinese ping-pong players were accepted by the U.S. public as a good way to break the ice between two nations separated by decades of hostility. Baseball with Cuba would serve a similar purpose in bridging the gap between the Bay of Pigs and a new relationship with Castro," read a secret memorandum prepared for Kissinger.[9]

On February 24, 1975, the game was called off by Kissinger, and Kuhn transmitted this decision to Cuban baseball officials. Over the next year, Kuhn persisted in his efforts for a series with the Cubans. "The purpose of the trip would be to engender cordial relations between baseball in Cuba and in the United States. There would be no political aspect or purpose,"[10] wrote Kuhn. A game scheduled for March 1976, which was to have been televised by ABC, was canceled when Kissinger was angered by Cuba's military involvement in the Angolan civil war.[11]

Chicago White Sox owner Bill Veeck made a quick trip to Cuba to evaluate talent in 1977. Although he returned convinced that Cuban players were not going to be available to the major leagues, he was optimistic about the possibilities of an exhibition game.

When President Jimmy Carter took office in January 1977, U.S.-Cuba relations encountered a four-year period of semithawing, and the travel ban was lifted for a brief period. In March 1977, newly appointed Secretary of State Cyrus Vance said he thought visits by U.S. athletes to Cuba would be constructive and promised a prompt decision regarding a proposed visit by the New York Yankees to Cuba in April.[12] If Fidel had had his way, the *New York Times* headline might have read, "Yankees Land in Havana as Mr. Castro Awaits with Open Arms."

"Before the Carter opening Castro had mentioned, several times in fact, that he really would like to have the Yankees come down and play against the Cuban national team," recalled Wayne Smith who, as the head of the U.S. Interests Section in Havana at the time, was the

United States's top diplomat in Cuba. Smith was first assigned to the U.S. embassy in Havana in 1958 and was also there when the embassy boarded its windows and closed in 1961. "With the Carter opening, having an American major league team go to Cuba seemed natural. But Bowie Kuhn put the skids to the Yankees going down, saying it would not be fair in that it would give the Yankees an advantage in recruiting. He thought it would be better to put together an all-star team," Smith told me.[13]

"If our government is in favor of it, I don't see how he [Kuhn] could stop a team from going," said Yankees owner George Steinbrenner who, in 1977, made a trip to Cuba to meet with sports officials. "If no players are going to come out, then no team can get a jump on the talent there." And New York Yankees president Gabe Paul, the man responsible for the last major league game in Cuba in 1959, was miffed because it was obvious the Cubans wanted to face the Yankees, not an all-star team.[14]

When the Cubans stated that no team would have an advantage in recruiting because they were not interested in selling their players, Kuhn responded by stating there would be no games if Cuban players were not free to negotiate contracts to play in the United States. Clearly Kuhn was receiving pressure from others, especially Los Angeles Dodgers owner Walter O'Malley, to prevent the Yankees from going.[15]

The idea of a game against a Cuban team was resuscitated in 1978. Gabe Paul, now Cleveland Indians team president, had proposed to play three exhibition games against a Cuban team in Tucson, Arizona, during the first week of April. Kuhn referred the decision to Major League Baseball's executive council. By the end of March, the commissioner's office had taken no action on the request, Kuhn had offered no comment, and the games were not played.[16] Smith remembers that Kuhn had received mixed signals from the Carter administration, with the State Department favoring the games, while the National Security Council was opposed.

In May 1978, it was announced in Cuba that *equipo Cuba* would play against the Montreal Expos in Montreal that August, but the game was canceled in July reportedly over a failure to reach agreement over television rights. In 1982, the Seattle Mariners canceled a spring exhibition game against a Cuban team. Mariners president Dan O'Brien, Sr., said it was pressure from Cuban Americans and not Kuhn that caused the game to be called off. "They just brought up the usual things about the placement of missiles in Cuba aimed at American cities and wondering how we could be part of it. We felt it was in the best interest not to stir that situation up," said O'Brien.[17]

Cuban fans mention Milwaukee, Texas, and California as other teams that made attempts to play in Cuba.[18] In 1997 and 1998, the Baltimore Orioles requested permission to go to the island and were denied on both occasions by the Treasury Department. In February 1999, the Anaheim Angels put their hat in the ring once again, asking the U.S Treasury Department for a license that would allow club officials to travel to Cuba to negotiate a game. Preston Gómez is a special assistant to the general manager of the Angels.

Disagreements between U.S. government agencies, disputes among the owners of major league teams, and protests from Cuban Americans had thwarted any efforts at baseball diplomacy. The central figure for many of these efforts was Commissioner Bowie Kuhn, who would have the last word in the form of a 1977 directive: "No discussion or negotiation with anyone in Cuba regarding the signing of any player to a professional contract is permitted. When and if Cuban players become available, an orderly system will be created for the allocation of player talent."[19]

The Kuhn Directive is still in effect at the turn of the century.

Astros 1977 Havana Trip

While no U.S. team had played a game in Cuba since 1959, the Houston Astros did go to Cuba in late 1977 for a series of clinics in Havana. Astros president Tal Smith, then the club's general manager, remembers being in the office of a Cuban sports official who asked, "Do you want to say hello to Fidel?" The official handed the phone to Smith, who was greeted by the *comandante en jefe*. Castro expressed his hopes that the trip was going well and apologized for not meeting with the Astro delegation, but he assured Smith that he would see that all their needs were met.[20]

Smith's interest in Cuba dates back to 1958 when he worked in minor league development for the Cincinnati Reds, who had a working agreement with Bobby Maduro and the Cuban Sugar Kings.

The 1977 trip was arranged by Dave LeFevre, who later was part of the ownership group led by John McMullin that bought the Houston team in 1979. LeFevre was also the person who told the New York Yankees in 1977 that Fidel was interested in having them play in Cuba.[21] "Dave and I had established a relationship when I was with the Yankees," said Smith. "He was a lawyer in New York and his maternal grandfather was Cyrus Eaton, and Cyrus Eaton had an association with Castro. We were able to do this through Dave's contacts at the State Department and in Cuba."

The Astros contingent included manager Bill Virdon, coaches Mel Wright, Deacon Jones, and Bob Lillis, and players Bob Watson, Ken Forsch, and Enos Cabel. Virdon played in the Cuban winter league in 1955, and Lillis was on the Dodger team that played in Havana in 1959. The players and coaches spent a week in Cuba conducting clinics, working with the Cuban national team, and watching games at the Estadio Latinoamericano. Many Cuban fans recall seeing those clinics. One of those fans is Asdrubal Baró, who played in the U.S. minor leagues in the 1940s and 1950s, including a stint with the Double A Houston Buffs in 1956.

Tal Smith did not tell Commissioner Kuhn that the Astros were going to Cuba because he didn't want to get turned down. "It was quite an experience. It was done on the spur of the moment because I felt that if we made a lot of noise about this before we went down, there would be somebody who would find a reason for us not to do it."

"Our interest was, of course, in getting a firsthand look at the Cuban talent, try to establish a relationship, and to foster that relationship in the event that the situation would open up in the future," said Smith.

Real Baseball Diplomacy

Wayne Smith, then chief of the U.S. diplomatic mission in Havana, recalls a small but telling event at a 1979 international baseball tournament during a particularly tense moment in U.S.-Cuba relations. "When the American team came on to the field, the 'Star-Spangled Banner' was played, and the Cuban crowd stood in silent respect." A Cuban fan leaned over and whispered to Smith: "You can't raise your flag over us by force, but you can through baseball."[22]

Cuban fans have great respect for U.S. players who outduel their own heroes, and none more than for Jim Abbott, who defeated the Cuban team in Havana in 1987. "Jim Abbott is so popular," one fan told me, "that if the Cuban government had any money, it would erect a statue to him."

In 1991, "Welcome Home Desert Storm" signs were raised next to the "Welcome Cuban Baseball Team" banners in the motel where *equipo*

Cuba was housed in Millington, Tennessee, just north of Memphis. This small town opened its arms and hearts to *equipo Cuba*, the pride and joy of the United States' number one enemy. The fans stood silently while the Cuban national anthem played and a Cuban flag, shipped express from the Cuban Interests Section in Washington, flew above the Olympic training site.

The people of Millington, many of whom were stationed or worked at the Memphis Naval Air Station at the time, were genuinely interested in becoming acquainted with their guests. A journalist pressed into service as a translator strained to comprehend the visitors' rapid Cuban Spanish and the hosts' Southern drawl. But there was no need to translate the smiles on both sides. I remember Cuban second baseman Antonio Pacheco, in the on-deck circle, motioning to the young U.S. batboy (the two did not speak each other's language) to share with him a folding chair reserved for players.

The reality is that while the two governments are at loggerheads, Cubans and U.S. citizens like each other—in part because of baseball. The tournament in Millington was baseball diplomacy at its best. "We need to stop the Cold War with Cuba. We need to break that barrier down, and we can start with baseball," said Dick Case, then executive director of the United States Baseball Federation, the national body representing all amateur baseball, told me. Case was the mastermind behind the annual USA-Cuba baseball series that was held each summer between 1986 and 1996. Mr. Case would make a fine diplomat.

"Several years ago we decided that to beat Cuba in baseball we had to play them head to head on a regular basis," explained Case. "I called Mr. Morales of the Cuban Baseball Federation. He said they wanted to set up an exchange to share ideas. It was in the best interest of both countries. They know that we are not after their players," said Case.

The Cuban team was set to make an eight-game tour in July 1997 but canceled the day they were supposed to arrive. Although there was much speculation that the Cubans were concerned about defections, the cancellation came on the same day that two bombs exploded in Havana hotels. And when the Cuban team turned down an invitation to go to Tucson, Arizona—the new USA Baseball headquarters—to play a five-game series against Team USA in the summer of 1998, it appeared unlikely that this form of baseball diplomacy would continue.

"I think baseball can be very useful. It is a passion we share, and that the Cubans don't share with any other major country," observed

Wayne Smith. "Obviously, without the will on both sides to move in the direction of a better relationship, baseball can't do much to bridge the gap. But given some will, baseball can help because it is something we have in common." But no matter how much goodwill exists on both sides, the U.S. embargo of Cuba remains a structural impediment to improved relations between the two countries.

The Embargo

Few baseball fans know or care much about the embargo, but it is the fundamental barrier impeding improved baseball relations between Cuba and the United States. Imposed unilaterally in 1962 in an attempt to pressure Fidel Castro out of government, it would appear that it has been a failure. Nine U.S. presidents and forty years later, Castro is still in power, and almost every country in the world trades with Cuba—except the United States.

On July 8, 1963, the U.S. government issued the Cuban Assets Control Regulations under the Trading with the Enemy Act. The regulations are administered by the U.S. Treasury Department's Office of Foreign Assets Control. "The basic goal of the sanctions is to isolate Cuba economically and deprive it of U.S. dollars," reads an overview of the regulations published by the Treasury Department.[23] In practical terms, this means no U.S. baseball organization is allowed to engage in any transactions with Cuba unless it requests a specific license. No club may enter into contractual relations with Cuba or Cuban nationals. And if a Cuban ballplayer signed a multimillion-dollar contract with a U.S. team, he would be prohibited from sending money home to Cuba without a Treasury Department license. The maximum penalties for ignoring U.S. government rules are ten years in prison and a $250,000 fine.

With the passage of the Helms-Burton legislation in 1996, President Clinton gave up his authority to change policy on Cuba without the approval of both houses of Congress. No representative or senator wants to be known as having given in to Castro—a charge they would surely face in a reelection bid.

The Cuban government's position of not allowing baseball players to sign professional contracts also presents a problem for renewed contact between Cuba and Major League Baseball. "Until Fidel dies, I don't see any way that would allow Cuban players to become professional," said Dihigo. "And now with Helms-Burton, *menos* [less]! *Menos!* During all these years, the Helms-Burton law and the embargo have served to strengthen the Cuban Revolution. It has not weakened it because the people have united behind nationalism, the same theme that Cubans rallied around against the Spanish over one hundred years ago," added Dihigo.

While there has been a great deal of discussion regarding "baseball diplomacy," especially in the wake of "ping-pong diplomacy" with China during the Nixon administration, there has really never been any serious effort at using baseball to ease the tension between the United States and Cuba. Both countries have attempted to use baseball as a weapon to gain some advantage over the other. Fidel has long harbored the idea that he can defeat his principal enemy at their own game. U.S. administrations from Eisenhower to Clinton have utilized baseball as a political tool, never as a move toward a real thawing of relations.

I recalled the words of sports talk radio producer Pedro Cruz González when I asked why major league baseball could not be discussed on his show. "*Es parte de la bronca* [It is part of the donnybrook]," he answered. *La bronca* is the best way to describe the impasse between the two countries. In both countries, any interest in or close relations with the other are viewed with suspicion. *La bronca* explains why U.S. Customs agents at the Miami airport harangue and hassle legal travelers to Cuba, and why Cuban academics who study the United States are not allowed to communicate with the U.S. Interests Section in Havana. *La bronca* simply reflects forty years of hostile relations between the United States and Cuba during which the two governments have used their hatred of each other to define the relationship. Baseball is indeed, *parte de la bronca.*

10 ☆ Beyond the Embargo and Fidel

In a meeting with U.S. newspaper editors in 1998, Fidel proposed "that Cuba be allowed to field two-major league teams and be given a share of the financial action when players leave their homeland to join clubs in the United States."[1] What was an off-the-cuff remark by Fidel was clarified a few days later by INDER head, Humberto Rodríguez. "We are receptive to any proposal by the major leagues as long as it respects the principles of Cuban socialist sports."[2]

Cuban government officials harbor absurd notions of Major League Baseball and the United States. Many continue to believe that race relations in the United States are frozen in 1959 and that black and Latino players in the big leagues face intolerable situations on a day-to-day basis. They also believe that Major League Baseball would grant a franchise to Cuba, allow the team to be composed only of Cuban players, and allow the Cuban government to keep all the money (there is no discussion where the government would come up with the cost of a franchise).

But the reality is that the Cuban government does not have the slightest interest in a major league franchise. "Havana does not want to run the ideological risk of contact between Cuban players and multimillionaire stars such as Kevin Brown or Mike Piazza," wrote *El Nuevo Herald* writer Jorge Morejón, probably the most astute observer of Cuban baseball in the United States.[3] The Cuban government knows that its so-called desire to have a major league club is so ludicrous that "they shout it to the four winds to give the impression that they are opening up to the world, when in reality any kind of opening would create a break in governmental control."

"If Cuba is really interested in opening itself to the world," writes Morejón, "it must permit their star players to come play in the United States and earn the money they deserve."

In 1996 and 1998, U.S. Congressman José Serrano (D-NY), who lives a block away from Yankee Stadium, proposed legislation that would allow Cuban baseball players to pursue their careers in the United States without having to defect.[4] Serrano's bill would allow the U.S. Immigration and Naturalization Service to grant work visas similar to those given to players from other countries.[5] Under current U.S. law, only Cuban defectors are allowed to play[6] and, claimed Serrano, Cubans are the only athletes required to defect in order to play in the United States.[7] "If a Cuban player comes to the United States and says, 'I have no problems with my country, with my government—I'm coming to play baseball,' then they won't let him play."

Some in Congress were opposed to the bill, fearing the Cuban government would confiscate the players' paychecks. And Serrano realized that the strong opposition from Cuban Americans Lincoln Díaz-Balart (R-FL), Robert Meléndez (D-NJ), and Ileana Ros Lehtinen (R-FL) insured that his bill failed.

If somehow an exception were made to U.S. policy to allow Cuban players to sign contracts with major league teams, what would happen to the money earned by the island's baseball stars? In the scenario envisioned by the Cuban government, it would take a large cut of the players' bonuses and salaries, in the same manner it does with players and coaches it contracts overseas. But this scenario is not likely to occur. Can anyone imagine Sammy Sosa giving 80 percent of his $10 million annual contract to the government of the Dominican Republic?

But the option that would present a serious challenge to the Cuban political system has the player bringing his money home to Cuba and deciding for himself how he will spend it. The concern of the Cuban government is that a player such as José Ariel Contreras might get a $10 million bonus from the Arizona Diamondbacks and return to Cuba sporting a Rolex while driving his new Bentley home to Pinar del Río. The money available to Cuba's baseball elite would make the flashy lifestyles of some of the Cuban musicians pale by comparison. And it would forever dispel the myth that Cuba, where the ever-growing disparity between those with access to dollars and those without continues to grow, retains its socialist character.

During eight years of investigating Cuban baseball, I dealt with every level of the game from players and fans, through coaches, trainers, and the office of the baseball commission itself. While Commissioner Carlos Rodríguez and other baseball officials did a reasonable job of reinvigorating the game on the island in the late 1990s, it is clear that most of the important decisions about baseball in Cuba are not made by the commissioner's office. There are three levels of decision-making above Commissioner Rodríguez.

One level is INDER, headed by Humberto Rodríguez. While some in Cuba viewed him as a young man willing to take risks, I saw no evidence of this. INDER's main function is to further political goals—to make the Revolution look good.

Above INDER is José Ramón "El Gallego" Fernández, the head of Cuba's Olympic Committee. Fernández, vice president of the Council of Ministries, was the field commander of the forces at Playa Girón (the Bay of Pigs), and is a close confidant of Fidel. Another decision-maker, parallel to Fernández, is José Ramón Balaguer, a member of the Central Committee of Cuba's Communist Party and the party's head of ideology. His responsibilities include relations with INDER. Balaguer is often quoted in the Cuban press when there is a need for a pep talk about moral incentives or the evils of professionalism. "When a man goes over to professionalism, he stops being independent, he is the property of the club's owner," says Balaguer.[8]

Above these two levels is Fidel, the owner of the club.

One of the main factors that has kept the Cuban government from moving away from its policy on professional baseball is the myth that *deporte es salud* (sport is health): that somehow athletes represent all that is good in the changes brought about by the Revolution. According to this myth, athletes set the example and, of course, are driven by moral incentives with no need for financial ones.

An additional motive for the Cuban government clinging to the amateur game is that Cuban baseball players hold high their country's flag wherever they go, and their medals are one of the few accomplishments the government can point to. As the Cuban economy entered a free fall, the government latched on to whatever it could for national pride and prestige. Baseball was the main asset. Whatever else, Cuba had the best amateur baseball team in the world.

But perhaps the most crucial factor in explaining why the Cubans do not want their star players going to the professional game is that most would end up in the United States. The best baseball in the world is played in the heart of the enemy. Early on, Fidel labeled professional baseball as *la pelota esclava* (slave baseball), as opposed to the new baseball in Cuba, which would be *la pelota libre* (free baseball). And the Cuban government clings hard to this image.

Instead of being regarded as diplomats, the players are treated with suspicion, spied upon, and expected to uphold some Spartan moral standard. The Cuban government argues that it can't allow baseball players to receive special treatment because it would not be fair to other sectors of society, such as doctors and university professors. But this privileged status already exists, and it is extended to those with access to U.S. dollars. The dollarization of the economy is the genie that cannot be made to return to the bottle.

"The Cuban government has to change its policy on baseball. Cuban baseball is at a crossroads. It's on the road to professionalism because there is no other road," explained Dihigo. "This government, or the next government, or the government in transition, *lo que sea* [whatever] has to guarantee liberty for people to choose what they want to do. When this happens, the baseball players will have an option."

Before the two countries can establish some semblance of a normal relationship in baseball, the United States must end its almost forty-year embargo of Cuba. Why does the United States keep the embargo after having failed to meet its original objective of driving Fidel from power? The most obvious answer is that the embargo is caught up in U.S. domestic political agendas, most of which involve the Cuban American community and the desire of both Democrats and Republicans to look tough on Cuba. But in addition to these domestic considerations, some U.S. policymakers view Fidel as more stable than other options at this moment. Cuba presents no real threat to the United States. We are not being swamped by immigration from Cuba, and the island is not a major haven for drug smugglers.

For the Havana regime, the most feared word is *transition*, and those in Cuba who publicly discuss any alternative to the current system are jailed. While the embargo has caused great hardships on the Cuban people, the Cuban government uses it as an excuse for any problem on the island. The embargo has helped Fidel maintain power and to reinsert state control in an period when it was eroding.

The United States could unilaterally end the embargo and initiate the process for the inevitable transformation in Cuba. No country in Latin America is more ready for real democracy—not the phony kind envisioned by the United States and detailed in the Helms-Burton law, where Cuban options would be limited by Washington and where huge influxes of outside money could determine the outcome of elections in favor of candidates favorable to the United States.

It is time for the governments of both Cuba and the United States to let the people of Cuba decide their own future. But with forces in both countries reaping domestic benefits from the embargo, don't look for its lifting anytime soon.

Ismael Sené, in his early sixties, is a fascinating man. He fought in the underground against the Batista regime and has held various government positions, including twenty years as a Cuban diplomat in Eastern Europe. After the fall of the socialist powers in Eastern Europe, Sené returned home to Cuba, where he worked in several government ministries. Finding these jobs less than challenging or exciting, he retired. Sené is a self-defined revolutionary, and an ardent baseball fan, and he is very concerned about the future of Cuban baseball.

For Sené, the fundamental problem is that players do not have access to dollars and do not earn enough pesos to make ends meet. "We have to give the players the opportunity to make money or we are going to lose them," said Sené. He then pointed to Cuban teams and sports figures earning money overseas. For the past several years, members of the women's volleyball team have received a very small percentage of tournament prize earnings—some of which can be as high as $1 million. Several of Cuba's top track-and-field stars have been contracted to Club Larios in Spain, with the contracts paid in dollars and the bulk of the money going to the Cuban government. The men's basketball team played in a professional tournament in Argentina, and the handball team played in Hungary.

Sené was particularly concerned about what he saw as a contradiction: the Cuban government was no longer wary of professionalism in sports, only of the effects of professionalism in sports on Cuban baseball. "The government even created a new ideological concept, *traidores al béisbol* [traitors to baseball]," said Sené. The reference was to a government announcement published in *Granma* banning several players for having contact with Rolando Arrojo and other players who had defected.

"And while some sports people here will complain about baseball players wanting to be professional, they get excited that Darcourt might be able to sign a professional contract with a French team," explained Sené, referring to Lázaro Darcourt, one of Cuba's few soccer stars.

In 1999, Cuba sent fifteen of its best soccer players (including Darcourt), all over age twenty-five, to play with Bonner, a fourth-division German club. The Cuban players will have an opportunity to receive instruction and to compete at a higher level, and the Germans will get a firsthand look at a new source of soccer talent. It is not inconceivable that if Germany begins to actively recruit Cuban players, young men on the island will begin to dream about the World Cup rather than the World Series.

"Few Cubans can tell you the name of the drummer from Los Van Van who can bring back dollars, but everyone can name all of the players on *equipo Cuba*. Why can musicians have dollars, and the baseball players cannot?" Sené asked rhetorically. "Because Fidel does not want it. Fidel says baseball players are the face of the Revolution."

Sitting at a table at the Casa de la Música with a tape of Los Van Van blaring in the background, I found it difficult to hear Mundo Pina, Van Van's trombone player, as we chatted before a concert in March 1998.

"I don't follow baseball in Cuba much any more," Pina told me. "The quality of play has diminished. Many players have retired, and others have been banned. This has taken away the Cubans' love of the game."

Taken away the love of the game? This is a serious charge. At first I thought Mundo didn't like baseball. I also thought it was the end of our conversation. But when a mutual friend mentioned to Mundo that I wrote about baseball, the musician's eyes opened wide, he moved his chair closer to mine, and began to shout in my ear to be heard over the din. Of the fifteen members of Los Van Van, Mundo is the biggest baseball fan.

Los Van Van and other musical groups tour outside of Cuba and then return home to play. I asked Mundo how it came to be that musical groups got to keep some of the money they earned overseas. "The government saw people like Arturo Sandoval stay abroad. And there was also a demand from the musical groups themselves," explains Pina. "I love Cuba and I want to live here." Obviously being able to bring home a few dollars makes his life a bit easier. Clearly the policy of allowing the musicians to keep some of their dollars works.

Why not let baseball players do the same? I asked. "The INDER people are to the left. They are the ones upholding the gains of the Revolution." He clearly felt this was an area where it would not be easy to modify policy. Cuban musicians had an advocate, the Minister of Culture, Abel Prieto, who was willing to take a risk. No one in INDER would dare do this.

Belling the Cat

One temporary solution—and Cuban baseball officials have certainly considered this—was to pay players. If a player could go to Italy or Japan and bring home $5,000, why not pay him $10,000 to stay and play in Cuba? This seemed like a very sound idea, and a way of directly confronting the players' lack of access to dollars. Several sources in Havana mentioned the play-for-pay proposal, and when I asked why the idea had not been adopted, I was told it had never been officially proposed. Why? *"Nadie quiere ponerle el cascabel al gato* [No one wants to bell the cat]," was the response. No one was willing to take the risk of crossing Fidel by proposing such a solution.

The phrase "belling the cat," comes from an Aesop's fable from around 600 B.C. In it, a group of mice decide that the best solution to stop the cat from eating them is to tie a bell around his neck. While all the mice agree this would be a wonderful solution, an old, wise mouse cautions them:

> Please pardon me.
> A bell on the cat would be lovely, indeed—
> Salvation both timely and fair—
> But one thing that worries this old head of mine:
> I'm wondering who'll put it there.
> Solutions to problems are easy, I vow,
> So long as you are not required to show how.[9]

The Return of Cubans to Major League Baseball

Was it Fidel's idea to sever Cuba's ties with U.S. professional baseball in the early 1960s or was he pressured into the decision by Major League Baseball and the U.S. government, which prohibited U.S. players and teams from competing in Cuba? The precise sequence of events will probably never be known and may be unimportant. It is, in essence, a variant of the "did Fidel become a Marxist or did the U.S. push him there" question. Ironically, it was the embargo, by limiting contact with the U.S. professional game, that allowed Cuba to develop the world's top amateur program.

Those interested in the return of Cuban players to major league baseball need to look to a Cuba without the embargo and without Fidel. Anything less means major league teams will be limited to exhibition games against *equipo Cuba*, and the only Cubans to play in the United States will be defectors.

Cuba is the largest producer of baseball players outside of the United States, and the U.S. major leagues are the top recruiters of players on the international market. It is only a matter of time before the supply and the demand come together. In the United States, there are not enough top-quality players available to major league baseball, while Cuba produces too many talented players for a twenty-four-man national team. Allowing Cuban players to compete in the United States would seem to be a logical solution to both problems. At some point in the future, and no one can provide a precise timetable, Cuban players will return to the U.S. professional game. And when they do, Cuba will quickly become the number one source of foreign-born players to professional baseball in the United States. U.S. fans will then have an idea of the depth of talent in Cuba, an understanding not possible from seeing only the trickle of players who have defected.

"I believe it would be great for Cubans to play in the major leagues, to earn money, and to receive the recognition they deserve," said Gilberto Dihigo. "It would also be good for Cuban fans. They could see Cubans in the big leagues as well as when the *peloteros* [ballplayers] return home to play in the winter. It would be good for everyone except Fidel."

In addition, Cuban athletes playing against better competition and receiving better instruction would also be available to represent their country in a World Cup or in the Olympics.[10] To accommodate this new arrangement, the Cubans would need to make only minor adjustments to the Serie Nacional schedule and arrange to have major league telecasts and broadcasts available for Cuban fans.

Other benefits to Cuban fans would be spring exhibition tours of major league teams, and the possibility that one or more teams would choose to locate their spring training headquarters in Cuba. Also, the Cuban baseball program would begin to interact with the cutting edge of baseball and to send their coaches to spring training camps in the United States.

In a post-embargo/Fidel future, U.S. organizations could establish facilities to recruit players throughout Cuba. The Cubans already have baseball academies—fifteen spread throughout the island. With a small investment in infrastructure, these could be used by U.S. organizations. Based on other teams' experiences—such as the Los Angeles Dodgers in the Dominican Republic or the Houston Astros in Venezuela—Cuba could greatly improve on its already outstanding baseball talent production.

How would Cuba regulate this new inclusion by Major League Baseball on the island? It could follow the pattern of the Mexican League, where clubs own the contracts of all Mexican-born players; the Dominican Republic, where teams have exclusive rights to a player for thirty days before having to sign him; or Venezuela, which has no regulations. But publicly at least, the Cuban government has given little thought to this subject. Just as it does not want its intellectuals to discuss options after Fidel and socialism, the old guard does not permit conjecture about possible future joint ventures with *la pelota esclava*. The future of Cuban baseball, like the future of the country itself, is integrally tied to the United States. The challenge for Cubans is to define how that relationship would function.

The Commissioner's Office of Major League Baseball is also aware that Cuba will open up, but it has no plan for dealing with this eventuality. Clearly, there must be an orderly process established if Cubans are allowed to sign U.S. professional contracts. Those who run Major League Baseball believe that if and when the market opens, there will be some kind of draft to prevent big-market teams from dominating. It is likely that one day Havana will have a major league franchise, but this is in the distant future. When it does, the organization will operate like any other team in big league baseball.[11]

Even without fundamental changes in the political relations between the United States and Cuba, there will be more games between Cuban teams and U.S. professional players who, under changes in International Baseball Association (IBA) rules, are now allowed to compete in international competitions.

The first of these meetings occurred in the Pan American Games in Winnipeg in 1999. Cuba defeated the United States in the title game, but both teams will advance to the next Olympics. A major test for the Cubans will be the 2000 Olympic Games in Sydney. It is possible the Cubans will send a team to Australia not necessarily composed of its best players, but of players the government believes will not defect. Or it will send its best team and run the risk of having some players stay behind.

With the change in the position of the IBA, the line between professional and amateur players has been blurred to the point where Cuba could realistically be considered for admission to the Caribbean Baseball Federation, the governing body of winter league baseball. Composed of leagues in the Dominican Republic, Mexico, Puerto Rico, and Venezuela, the federation holds the annual Serie del Caribe each February. The series began in Havana in 1949 and featured Cuba, Panama, Puerto Rico, and Venezuela. The Cuban teams won seven of the first twelve tournaments, which ended in 1960. Under pressure from the U.S. government, the 1961 series, scheduled for Havana, was transferred to Venezuela without the Cubans being invited and then was canceled for financial reasons. After a ten-year hiatus, the series resumed in 1970 with teams from the Dominican Republic and Mexico replacing Cuba and Panama; with the exception of 1981, the series has since been held annually.

Cuba has expressed interest in again participating in the series but faces one serious obstacle: a rule of the Caribbean Baseball Federation that states that baseball in the member countries cannot be under government control. Because of the federation's agreement with Major League Baseball, Major League Baseball would also have to approve the return of the Cubans. Of course, as long as the embargo is in place, U.S. players would be prohibited from going to Cuba.

Although Cuba is in crisis, baseball will continue to thrive; it is part of the national culture, in a way that it is not in the United States. Kids still play stickball in cities and fields throughout the island. And baseball is clearly the sport of choice for young men who are physically talented, receive good basic instruction, play year-round, and are identified as prospects early.

It is necessary to distinguish between "national baseball," the 135-year tradition of the sport on the island, and "revolutionary baseball," the past forty years of amateur baseball in Cuba. Fidel has tried to connect Cuban nationalism with the Revolution. He has attempted to appropriate baseball for his political needs, for example by winning medals for Cuba. This blending of sport, nationalism, and the Revolution fits into his bigger social project of making sports available to all Cubans. While the Cuban government after 1959 did develop other sports, baseball has always been a part of Cuba, even before it was an independent country. Cuban nationalism is much deeper than the Revolution, and it is tied to baseball: baseball belongs to Cuba, not to Fidel. At the turn of the century, Fidel is still stuck on *la pelota esclava*—only now the slaves are the players trapped on the island. After the embargo is lifted and Fidel is gone, baseball will still be there, for it is indeed part of the soul of Cuba.

☆ Epilogue: From the Bay of Pigs to Baltimore

In January 1999, the Baltimore Orioles were given the green light by the U.S. Department of State to play two exhibition games against *equipo Cuba*. Although Orioles owner Peter Angelos had been requesting U.S. government permission to play in Cuba since 1996, this time he did not need to ask. The games were included as part of a Clinton administration foreign policy initiative.[1]

The White House rushed to get a package together to undercut a Republican proposal for a national commission to review and revise U.S. policy toward Cuba. It was thought that the commission, which included Henry Kissinger and Senator John Warner (R-VA), might call for an end to the embargo.[2] Why the move to undercut the commission? The most simplistic explanation is that the Clinton administration wanted to avoid offending the Cuban American communities in Florida and New Jersey, and thus aid Al Gore's chances of winning those states in the 2000 presidential elections.

The initiative was viewed by the Cubans as nothing new and was met with disdain in Havana. When examined closely, the policy announcement was in reality little more than an updated Platt Amendment, the turn-of-the-century instrument used by the United States to dominate internal Cuban politics after the country gained independence from Spain. Although rejecting most of what the United States proposed, the Cuban government left open the possibility of the encounters with the Orioles.

Angelos led a twelve-person delegation, including Sandy Alderson, executive vice-president of baseball operations for Major League Baseball, to Cuba in mid-January. Agreement was reached on all technical and procedural aspects: games would be played on March 28 in Havana and April 3 in Baltimore, improvements would be made to the stadium in Havana, and the teams would use wooden bats. The one glitch was the disposition of the proceeds from ticket sales and television rights. The United States wanted the money to go to Catholic Charities in Cuba. The Cubans, finding this an unacceptable intrusion into their internal affairs, suggested the money buy medical supplies for the Cuban doctors treating victims of Hurricane Mitch in Central America.

I landed in Havana only two days after the Orioles visit had been proposed. Baseball fans were excited, though restrained in their expectations because they had been disappointed on so many occasions in the past. They also feared that tickets would be given out only to government supporters, or worse, sold to foreign tourists.

"On January 17, part of the Orioles delegation showed up unexpectedly at El Latino [Estadio Latinoamericano] and gave out quite a few baseball caps to the fans," Marcelo Sánchez wrote to me. "They are going to have a press conference tomorrow to announce the possibility of the March game, but I tell you I'm pessimistic. I hope I'm wrong."[3] Marcelo was wrong. When it appeared the game would be called off, the United States and Cuba reached an agreement for two games, the first to be played in Havana on March 28 and the second in Baltimore in May. Profits from the games and television rights would go only to baseball programs in the United States and Cuba. After forty years, a major league team was going to Cuba.

About fifteen minutes before the first pitch of the March 28 game in Havana, Fidel stepped onto the field along the third base line and briskly walked over to the Orioles dugout. He was dressed in fatigues and cap, and his presence filled the entire stadium. The handpicked crowd broke into polite applause, then a short chant of "Fi-del", Fi-del." Once Fidel was in full stride, an announcement was made on the public address system. "Attention fans: *el Primer Secretario del Comité Central del Partido Comunista de Cuba y Presidente de los Consejos de Estado y Ministros* has just made his entrance," and after a pause, "*Nuestro Comandante en Jefe*, Fidel Castro Ruz."

As one Cuban journalist put it, "When Fidel walked onto the field before the game, it ceased to be a baseball game and became a Fidel event." But Castro's imprint on the game was evident long before he appeared at the stadium. He determined who would play on the Cuban squad, and he set the policy of who would be allowed into the stadium. This was Fidel at his classic best. He was in absolute control. With the game in Havana, the Cuban government had the opportunity to put its best players on the field and show a U.S. television audience some of baseball's most passionate fans. It chose to do neither.

After spending a few minutes with the Orioles, Fidel marched back across the field, greeted the Cuban players, and then entered the grandstands and waved to the crowd. He settled into a front-row box with baseball commissioner Bud Selig on his left and Peter Angelos on his right. Fidel did not do the wave, but he did stand at attention for the "Star Spangled Banner."

Most Cuban fans did not have the opportunity to see the game in person. But the game was shown on national television (between innings, viewers saw an announcement condemning the Helms-Burton law), and the streets of Havana were empty. Admission to the game was by invitation only, and ticket distribution was limited to Communist Party faithful, "exemplary workers," and students. Many of those invited were not baseball fans. Fidel tried to pass off this domesticated group to Baltimore manager Ray Miller as "the best fans in the world." But it was clear that Fidel Castro wanted a tame crowd, rather than the high-intensity fans who had packed the Estadio Latinoamericano on the two previous nights. The constant sound of drums, air horns, and chatter of the fans, along with dancing in the aisles, provided an electric atmosphere for the first two games of the play-offs between the hometown Industriales and cross-island arch-rival Santiago.

The Baltimore game was a sort of lull in what may have been the most exciting week in contemporary Cuban baseball. The Industriales defeated Isla de la Juventud on Tuesday and Wednesday before packed houses at the Estadio Latinoamericano to move to the finals. On Friday and Saturday, the Industriales defeated Santiago in the first two games of the championship series. While the crowds were large, some fans stayed away in protest of the invitation-only format for the Orioles game. Still, the four games combined drew well over two hundred thousand fans.

The Baltimore game, which started slowly, picked up intensity as the Cubans demonstrated they could go head-to-head with the Orioles' opening-day line-up (minus Cal Ripken, who stayed home because of the death of his father). For a game in which Cuban hitters had to adjust to both using wooden bats and facing major league pitching, it was a very impressive performance, and the Cuban team gained the respect not only of the Orioles but of representatives of more than twenty-five other teams who attended the game.

Omar Linares carried the Cuban flag in pregame ceremonies, and then he almost carried his team. His RBI single in the eighth tied the game at 2–2, but in the tenth with runners on first and second, he popped out to left. The Cubans missed the bat of all-time home run leader Orestes Kindelán, the fielding and leadership of second baseman Antonio Pacheco, and the acrobatics of shortstop Germán Mesa. All three, along with half a dozen other key players, were not included on the roster because their teams were still in the play-offs.

But the Cuban team, which was referred to as *selección Cuba*, not *equipo Cuba*, did include the island's top pitchers, the best of whom is twenty-seven-year-old José Ariel Contreras. The 6'3", 225-lb. Contreras came in as relief in the second inning and pitched eight scoreless innings while giving up only two hits and striking out ten batters. He fanned Albert Belle twice, including once after he walked Will Clark intentionally to face him. It was the first time Contreras had ever faced hitters with wooden bats in a game situation. Contreras showcased himself in what may have been the most widely seen tryout camp in the history of baseball.

The game, which went into extra innings, was won by Baltimore 3–2. The difference was a two-run homer in the second inning by Orioles catcher Charles Johnson who eight years earlier, while playing in this same stadium for Team USA, was robbed of a game-winning hit by a magnificent play by Germán Mesa.

Inside the stadium, Johnson was flashing signs to pitcher Scott Erickson, and the Cuban coaches were signaling messages to their batters and base runners. Outside the stadium, Cubans were using gestures to refer to issues they prefer not to put into words: stroking imaginary beards on their chins or tapping their shoulders to indicate military insignias—both references to Fidel. Others formed imaginary hand puppets—a reference to informers—also known in Cuba as *chivatos* (literally meaning a small goat) or *trompetas* (trumpets), while still others made a motion of a key turning into the torso, a reference to the omnipresent state security apparatus.

At the Friday game between the Industriales and Santiago, I had my first encounter with Fidel's bodyguards, who had established a security perimeter around the stadium for the entire weekend. They do not smile, nor do they respond to any questions except to say "No." I saw a member of Cuba's baseball commission explaining to these elite guards why he should be allowed in the area behind home plate. I briefly chatted with Carlos Rodríguez and, at his suggestion, set up a meeting for the following morning. When I arrived at the appointed time, I was met by a stone-faced middle-aged man with glasses—I assumed he was one of Fidel's men—who refused to let me in to the hallway leading to the commissioner's office. I later found out that the disagreeable fellow was Reinaldo Calviak, the director of the International Press Center, who carries the rank of ambassador. At that moment, I finally understood what little power the baseball commissioner actually had.

At a press conference on Monday following the game, Ricardo Alarcón, president of the National Assembly and one of Cuba's top government officials, was asked to explain the difference between the Baltimore-Cuba game and ping-pong diplomacy with China.

"More than ping-pong, it was the discovery by the United States of the People's Republic of China, a country which had normal relations with so many other countries. I am certain that something similar will happen with Cuba, I just don't know when it will happen," said Alarcón. "I don't know how many baseball games we will have to play until we reach that day, but we are ready to wait until it happens. But if it takes many games, I hope we win most of them."

Alarcón then returned to his favorite theme: the embargo. "Rather than ask about a special agreement in baseball between the U.S. and Cuba, you have to ask others how long this abnormal relationship will exist," said Alarcón.

Back to the *Esquina Caliente*

I found the Orioles-Cuba game depressing. Fidel had never been more transparent in attempting to appropriate Cuban national identity for his own political purposes. On that Sunday afternoon, he tried to steal the soul of Cuba. Fidel sat through the entire game schmoozing with Bud Selig and Peter Angelos while Major League Baseball remained taboo for the Cuban media. I needed to check my impressions with

Cuba's real fans and my friends at the Peña Deportiva Parque Central. During the two days before the Orioles game, film, video crews, and reporters had to take a number at the park as several hundred members of the foreign media descended on Havana and the *esquina caliente* became an obligatory stop.

In the park, some argued over strategy used in the Baltimore-Cuba game while others replayed the Mark McGwire–Sammy Sosa home run race, which had been the buzz of Havana the previous summer and fall. There had been no mention of the home run kings in the Cuban media, but government bureaucrats working at the main radio and television building had seen each of McGwire's and Sosa's at bats. At the same time, in a two-room apartment in the center of Havana, a dozen men gathered around an old console radio listening to baseball broadcasts from Miami; when the police discovered the radio, it was confiscated.

Over lunch, Marcelo Sánchez explained that he had met with more than twenty reporters in a three-day period but did not receive an invitation to the game. Nor did anyone else from the Peña except Asdrubal Baró, who attended with a group of professional players. Even though they were excluded, Marcelo and the others viewed the event as enhancing the possibility of better relations between the United States and Cuba.

Marcelo introduced me to a man in his mid-fifties who described himself as a passionate baseball fan. The Pope's visit was important, he said, and it was nice that Christmas had been restored as a holiday but, he announced, henceforth he would measure time in "before" and "after" the Orioles' visit to Cuba. He added that the Orioles game gave hope to several generations of Cubans who followed major league baseball. "What's next?" I asked. He hesitated for a moment. Then with a smile, he responded, "It depends on what moves the two managers make," alluding to the U.S. and Cuban governments.

Selección Cuba Visits Baltimore

On May 3, as Baltimore was mired in the cellar of the American League East, the *selección Cuba* visited Camden Yards. The three hundred members of the Cuban delegation included several former professional ballplayers, including Ernesto "Chico" Morilla, the man who struck out Stan Musial. While watching the game on television, I spotted Chico holding a huge Cuban flag in the seats behind the third base dugout. It was obvious that many of the Orioles players simply did not want to play on what would have been a rare off day. The Orioles looked dreary, particularly Albert Belle, who watched eleven consecutive pitches sail by and struck out twice. This game meant nothing to most of the Orioles players, and their less-than-professional performance showed it.

On the other hand, the game was very important to the Cubans. Although there was no mention made in the U.S. press, the head of the Cuban delegation to Baltimore was José Ramón "El Gallego" Fernández, the field commander of the Cuban troops at Playa Girón. Now he was leading the Cubans into combat again. The Cubans played with intensity and passion while pounding out eighteen hits in a 12–6 win. Omar Linares reached base in every plate appearance, going four for four with two walks. Even though Baltimore played dismally, the game showed the Cubans could compete against major leaguers. The Cuban victory may have been the most important game of *béisbol revolucionario*. The next day *Granma* had a one word headline: *¡Ganamos!* (We Won!).[4]

The Cubans boarded their charter early the next morning for the return to Havana. At 6:30 A.M., cars with loud speakers began cruising the streets of the Cuban capital urging everyone to get out to the University of Havana to welcome back the team. "The pomp and circumstance of military pageant were now reserved for victorious athletes, disciplined like soldiers, who would proudly carry national flags," notes Roberto González Echevarría in his book *The Pride of Havana*.[5] The troops were returning home after a major victory overseas.

Fidel was at the airport to embrace team captain Omar Linares. "Dear commander-in-chief, the mission you gave us has been completed," exclaimed Linares, ending his battle report to the *comandante en jefe* with the words *¡Socialismo o muerte!* (Socialism or death!) *¡Patria o muerte!* (Homeland or death!) *¡Venceremos!* (We will triumph!)

The entourage proceeded to the University of Havana, where Fidel gave a three-hour speech (which, for the players, must have made the fifty-six-minute rain delay in Baltimore seem like a brief interlude). Fidel viewed the game as a battle between two concepts of sport: one played by professionals for money and the other played by Cubans for the love of game and country. In terms of his forty-year battle with the United States, this may have been Fidel's most important moment in direct confrontation with his northern neighbor since the victory at the Bay of Pigs. He had defeated the *yanquis* at their own game.

Using military terms, he charged that the United States was trying to buy off Cuban athletes: "*Esa es la primera batalla* [That's the first battle]," "*la lucha contra esos bandidos llamados scouts* [the fight against those bandits called scouts]." Fidel stressed the fact that no players had defected in Baltimore.[6] He did not discuss the inherent contradiction implicit in facing a major league team: the Cubans showcased their players to Major League Baseball and instilled in them the confidence that they can compete at that level.

Fidel alluded to Cuban musicians earning dollars and commented that if one day there are normal relations with the United States, the players could be paid more. Another example of Fidel blaming the embargo and holding out the hope of a better future. Fidel then explained how he conceived the difference between the two exhibition games against Baltimore. Winning the game in Havana was not important, said Fidel. The purpose it served was to show U.S. visitors (and I assume those watching on television) that Cuban fans were very respectful and that *Cuba no es un pueblo de salvajes* (Cubans are not savages). This helps to explain his handpicked crowd.

"The game we have to win is there," said Fidel. In the two weeks leading up to the Baltimore game, he was a frequent visitor—some reports say daily—to the team practices at the Estadio Latinoamericano. Fidel noted how he asked the manager and coaches detailed questions related to baseball strategy. Baseball commissioner Rodríguez reported that the players were inspired by the *comandante en jefe*'s presence. I recalled the words of González Echevarría: "A manager calling for a steal or to stay out of a double play is like a general planning a battle."[7] In the preparations for the Baltimore trip, Fidel was Billy Martin and George Steinbrenner all rolled into one.

"In a couple of weeks, the troops will gather again to fight for a position on *equipo Cuba*," said Fidel. The next battle would be in Winnipeg for the Pan American Games, and then, he hoped, on to Sydney for the 2000 Olympic games.

The comments of Major League Baseball officials notwithstanding, the Baltimore-Cuba encounters were political. While some observers saw the games as an example of "baseball diplomacy," there are no indications that either side softened their hard-line positions or that either the United States or Cuba cares about an immediate change in the relationship. We are no closer to improved relations between the two governments than we were before the games were played. I don't use the word *normalization* because the United States and Cuba have never had normal relations during Cuba's almost one-hundred-year history.

But the games may have begun to loosen the ground in the United

States that underlies the embargo policy. The U.S. public saw a group of talented, proud, and passionate baseball players and had to wonder how much of a threat Cuba could be to the United States in a post-Soviet era. But the reverse was true in Cuba. Defeating a major league team only reaffirmed the Cuban government's convictions that their system works. And Fidel softened his image in the United States at a time when his regime has never been more repressive toward internal opposition at home. There is talk of having four big league teams go to Cuba in the spring of 2000. This would be great for baseball, and even better for Fidel.

As the man in the Parque Central told me, a thawing of U.S.-Cuba relations depends on the moves of the managers. Fidel, Cuba's owner-manager, understands how to use baseball to achieve his political goals. He is at his best when he is in combat. So while Cuba is facing a full count, Fidel waits for the next pitch from the United States.

NOTES
BIBLIOGRAPHY
INDEX

NOTES

1. Cuban Baseball and the United States

1. Wayne Smith, *The Closest of Enemies* (New York: W. W. Norton, 1987), 13–14.

2. Louis A. Pérez, Jr., *Between Revolution and Reform*, 2d ed. (New York: Oxford University Press, 1995), 290, 313.

3. Marifeli Pérez-Stable, *The Cuban Revolution: Origins, Course, and Legacy* (New York: Oxford University Press, 1993), 53.

4. Eugene McCarthy, "Diamond Diplomacy," *New Republic*, 28 April 1982, 12.

5. U.S. Senate Select Committee to Study Governmental Operations with Respect to Intelligence Activities, *Alleged Assassination Plots Involving Foreign Leaders* (Washington, D.C.: U.S. Government Printing Office, 1975), 73.

2. "It Begins with the Dreams of Their Fathers": Baseball and National Identity in Cuba

1. See John Holway, *Blackball Stars: Negro League Pioneers* (Westport, Conn.: Meckler Books, 1988), which devotes a chapter to Martín Dihigo.

2. Roberto González Echevarría, *The Pride of Havana: A History of Cuban Baseball* (New York: Oxford University Press, 1999), 181.

3. Bruce Brown, "Cuban Baseball," *Atlantic*, 6 June 1984, 112. This is also cited in Rob Ruck, "Baseball in the Caribbean," in *Total Baseball*, 5th ed., ed. John Thorn et al. (New York: Viking Perennial, 1997), 475. Alfredo Santana Alonso, author of *El inmortal del béisbol: Martín Dihigo* (Havana: Editorial Científico-Técnica, 1988), says he could not confirm that Dihigo gave money to the expedition, so he excluded this incident in his book. Interview with

Santana Alonso in Ciego de Ávila, Cuba, March 8, 1998. The *Granma* was the yacht used by the Castro forces on their return to Cuba in 1956. After 1959, *Granma* was the name given to the official government newspaper in Cuba.

4. See also Roberto González Echevarría, "The Game in Matanzas: On the Origins of Cuban Baseball," *Yale Review* 83, no. 3 (1995): 62–94; Louis A. Pérez, Jr., "Between Baseball and Bullfighting: The Quest for Nationality in Cuba, 1868–1898," *Journal of American History* 81, no. 2 (1994): 493–517; Rob Ruck, *The Tropic of Baseball: Baseball in the Dominican Republic* (Westport, Conn.: Meckler, 1991), 2–3.

Pérez and González Echevarría concur with Gilberto Dihigo's comments. "Baseball arrived in colonial Cuba at a critical moment in the formation of national identity, even as the Cubans were assembling the distinct elements that defined a separate nationality," states Pérez ("Between Baseball and Bullfighting," 494). "The origins of Cuban baseball coincided with independence from Spain and with the consolidation of national identity," writes González Echevarría ("The Game in Matanzas," 62). "Growing up Cuban meant growing up with baseball. In most instances there was no consciousness of the American origin of the game. Baseball had been played ever since there was a nation, hence it was part of the nation" (94). The Pérez article and the González Echevarría book *The Pride of Havana* provide extensive detail on the origins of Cuban baseball and its connections to Cuban nationalism.

5. For detail on Sabourín, see Pérez, "Between Baseball and Bullfighting," 514, and accompanying footnotes.

6. Pérez, "Between Baseball and Bullfighting," 505.

7. Angel Torres, *La leyenda del béisbol cubano* (Los Angeles: the author, 1997), 6. Gabino Delgado and Severo Nieto, *Béisbol cubano: récords y estadísticas* (Havana: Editorial Lex, 1955), 163. It seems clear that Cuban baseball had more than one father, with Guilló, Bellán, and Sabourín all apparently able to share this distinction.

In addition to the lack of solid facts about Guilló, there seems to be a bit of confusion. Paula J. Pettavino and Geralyn Pye, in *Sport in Cuba: The Diamond in the Rough* (Pittsburgh: University of Pittsburgh Press, 1994), 26, state: "The first modern bat and ball were brought to Cuba in the 1860s by Nemesio Guillot [sic], an upper-class Cuban who had been studying at Fordham University in New York. Other students studying in the United States, as well as North American businessmen and sailors, helped to introduce and spread baseball throughout the island. In 1866, a U.S. ship crew played a team of Cuban stevedores in an exhibition game." Their source for the information on Guilló was Eric A. Wagner, "Baseball in Cuba," *Journal of Popular Culture* 18, no. 1 (1984). Wagner, citing Luis Hernández, describes Guilló as "a Cuban who had studied abroad." Wagner does not mention Fordham. The Hernández article states that the first bat and ball appeared in Cuba in 1864.

"They were brought by Nemesio Guillot [sic], a Cuban who studied abroad" (Luis Hernández, "Un siglo de béisbol en Cuba," *Semanario Deportivo LPV*, 2 December 1969, 8).
   Pettavino and Pye also cite Michael M. Oleksak and Mary Adams Oleksak, *Béisbol: Latin Americans and the Grand Old Game* (Grand Rapids, Mich.: Masters Press, 1991), 5–6, which in its mention of Guilló cites Joseph L. Arbena, *Sport and Society in Latin America* (New York: Greenwood Press, 1988). But the Arbena book is an edited work, and the citation is really to another article by Eric A. Wagner, "Sport in Revolutionary Societies: Cuba and Nicaragua," in *Sport and Society in Latin America*, ed. Joseph L. Arbena (New York: Greenwood Press, 1988), 113–36. Wagner's source is the Hernández article. The Oleksaks state that Guilló returned home to Cuba in 1866; neither Arbena, nor Hernández, nor Wagner state this. The Oleksaks mention that Bellán studied at Fordham, and this is probably where the confusion begins.
   8. González Echevarría, *Pride of Havana*, 90. Drawn from a 1924 Cuban newspaper article that featured an interview with Guilló, this is the most reliable source of information.
   9. González Echevarría's *The Pride of Havana* is the most detailed source on Cuban baseball history available in either English or Spanish. There are at least two forthcoming works on Cuban baseball: Peter Bjarkman and Mark Rucker, *Smoke: The Romance and Lore of Cuban Baseball* (New York: Total Sports, 1999); and Peter Bjarkman, *Baseball and Castro's Revolution* (Jefferson, N.C.: McFarland, forthcoming). These three books provide much of the detail on Cuban baseball history and statistical information not included in this book.
   There are several useful books on Cuban baseball in Spanish. Torres, *La leyenda del béisbol cubano*, is like an almanac with advertisements. While the Torres book contains wonderful photos and interesting stories, there is very little about the period in Cuba after 1959. *Viva y en juego*, by Edel Casas, Jorge Alfonso, and Alberto Pestana (Havana: Ministro de Cultura, Editorial Científico-Técnica, 1986), gives both historical context and statistics. Tom Miller, *Trading with the Enemy: A Yankee Travels Through Castro's Cuba* (New York: Atheneum, 1992) contains a interesting section on Cuban baseball.
   10. González Echevarría, *Pride of Havana*, 100.
   11. Pérez, "Between Baseball and Bullfighting," 503, 516.
   12. Roberto González Echevarría, "The '47 Dodgers in Havana: Baseball at a Crossroads," *1996 Spring Training Baseball Yearbook* 9 (Spring 1996): 20–25.
   13. U.S. House Subcommittee on Inter-American Affairs of the Committee on Foreign Relations, *Soviet Naval Activities in Cuba*, 91st Cong., 2nd sess., 26 September 1971, 12. Colonel Oliver North tried to use the same logic

to establish a Cuban presence in Nicaragua in the mid-1980s. During a briefing with NBC reporter Tom Brokaw, North showed a photo of a military camp in Nicaragua. "The interesting thing here is the baseball diamond. Nicaraguans don't play baseball. Cubans play baseball." North was unaware that baseball was introduced in Nicaragua at the turn of the century and was far and away the dominant sport of the country.

14. Ruck, "Baseball in the Caribbean," 474. See also Peter Bjarkman, *Baseball with a Latin Beat* (Jefferson, N.C.: McFarland, 1994), 236.

15. Adrian Burgos, Jr., "Jugando en el norte: Caribbean Players in the Negro Leagues, 1910–1950," *Centro: Journal of the Center for Puerto Rican Studies* 8, nos. 1 & 2 (1996): 136.

16. Pérez, "Between Baseball and Bullfighting," 514. Pérez's original source is Tirso A. Valdez, *Notas acerca del béisbol dominicano del pasado y del presente* (Ciudad Trujillo, Dominican Republic: Editorial del Caribe, 1958), 11. See also Casas et al., *Viva y en juego*, 113.

17. Pérez, "Between Baseball and Bullfighting," 515. See also Jess Losada, "Hace cuarenta y seis años se jugaba baseball en Caracas," *Carteles* (Havana), 30 November 1941, 8–9.

18. Gilbert M. Joseph, "Documenting a Regional Pastime: Baseball in Yucatán," in *Windows on Latin America: Understanding Society through Photographs*, ed. Robert M. Levine (Coral Gables, Fla.: North-South Center, University of Miami, 1987), 79. See also Luis Ramírez Aznar, *La historia del béisbol en Yucatán*, vol. 1 (Mérida, Mexico: Novedades, 1989), 9.

19. Bjarkman, *Baseball with a Latin Beat*, 27.

20. There is a great deal of material written on these early Cuban players. See works by Bjarkman and González Echevarría.

21. Severo Nieto told me that the expression *querido Cinci* began in 1911 when Almeida and Marsans made it to the big leagues, but it really took hold with the success of Luque in the 1920s.

Cincinnati played exhibition games in Havana in 1908, which led to the signing of Almeida and Marsans, and eventually Luque (González Echevarría, *Pride of Havana*, 336). González Echevarría also points out that the Cuban Sugar Kings in the 1950s were a Cincinnati farm club, helping to solidify the popularity of the club in Cuba. Cincinnati also had a working agreement with Marianao in the Cuban League during the 1940s and 1950s.

Martín Dihigo's son, and Gilberto's older brother, Martín, was signed to a minor league contract by the Cincinnati Reds in 1959. Although Martín Dihigo, Jr., never made it to the major leagues, his minor league career lasted until 1962.

22. Burgos has a detailed discussion of Caribbean players' racial identity and also documents Cuban players in the U.S. Negro Leagues and the role winter baseball—especially in Cuba—played in offering employment oppor-

tunities for U.S. Negro League players. See also Don Rogosin, *Invisible Men* (New York: Atheneum, 1987), especially Chapter 6, "The Latin Connection."

23. Manuel García received his nickname *Cocaína*—cocaine—because his fastball put batters to sleep; he was never involved in a drug-use scandal. García explained the derivation of his nickname when I interviewed him in Caracas in 1990.

24. Dick Clark and Larry Lester, eds., *The Negro Leagues Book* (Cleveland: Society for American Baseball Research, 1994), 119. Many U.S. black players went to Cuba. One of those, Willie Wells, won the MVP in 1938–39.

"Not Just Black: African Americans, Cubans and Baseball," by Lisa Brock and Bijan Bayne in *Between Race and Empire: African-Americans and Cubans before the Cuban Revolution*, eds. Lisa Brock and Digna Castañeda Fuertes (Philadelphia: Temple University Press, 1998), 186–204, provides detail on the experiences of black Cuban players in the United States and the interest of the African American community in those teams.

25. Thomas Boswell, *How Life Imitates the World Series* (New York: Penguin, 1983), 95.

26. Lloyd Johnson and Miles Wolff, eds., *The Encyclopedia of Minor League Baseball* (Durham, N.C.: Baseball America, 1993), 220–76.

27. This team is often incorrectly called the Havana Sugar Kings. There has never been a team named the Havana Sugar Kings. The Havana Cubans existed between 1946 and 1954, and the Cuban Sugar Kings between 1956 and 1960.

28. Jorge Alfonso and Enrique Capetillo, "Su pueblo ganó un gran conductor," *Bohemia*, 16 October 1987, 83.

29. Kevin Kerrane, *Dollar Sign on the Muscle* (New York: Simon & Schuster, 1984), 312.

30. David J. Truby, "Castro's Curveball," *Harper's*, May 1989, 32–33.

31. Tad Szulc, *Fidel: A Critical Portrait* (New York; William Morrow, 1987), 87.

32. Don Hoak with Myron Cope, "The Day I Batted Against Castro," *Sport*, June 1964, 30+.

33. Peter Bjarkman, "Baseball and Fidel Castro," *National Pastime: A Review of Baseball History* 18 (1998): 64–68. See also González Echevarría, *Pride of Havana*, 6.

34. Robert Quirk, *Fidel Castro* (New York: W. W. Norton, 1993), 4.

35. Casas et al., *Viva y en juego*, 220.

36. Gianni Miná, *Un encuentro con Fidel*. (Havana: Oficina de Publicaciones del Consejo de Estado, 1987), 301.

37. "Cuba's Boys of Summer," Cable News Network video on Cuban baseball, July 1996.

38. González Echevarría, *Pride of Havana*, 76.

39. Sonia Castanes, ed., *Fidel sobre el deporte*, (Havana: INDER, 1975), par. 368. Cited in R.J. Pickering, "Cuba", in *Sport under Communism*, ed. James Riordan (Montreal: McGill-Queen's University Press, 1978), 152.

3. Béisbol Revolucionario: *The Best Amateur Baseball in the World*

1. Rubén Rodríguez, "Serie Nacional y IX Festival," *Semanario Deportivo LPV*, 27 April 1965, 5; and "Oye . . . a la pelota," *Semanario Deportivo LPV*, 2 March 1965, 5. Amateur baseball was not new to Cuba in 1961, having been played alongside the professional game in Cuba for decades.

2. Steve Fainaru, "Revolutionary: Playing for the Love of the Game," *Boston Globe*, 3 December 1995.

3. "Cuba's Boys of Summer," Cable News Network video on Cuban baseball, July 1996.

4. Leonardo Padura and Raúl Arce, *El alma en el terreno: Estrellas del béisbol* (La Habana: Editorial Abril, 1989), 145.

5. Padura and Arce, *El alma en el terreno*, 149.

6. Padura and Arce, *El alma en el terreno*, 154.

7. Pettavino and Pye, *Sport in Cuba*, 70. This is the most comprehensive look at the Cuban sports programs available.

8. John Sugden, *Boxing and Society: An International Analysis* (Manchester: Manchester University Press, 1996), 164.

9. Tom Miller, "Cuba's All-Stars," *Natural History* 108, no. 33 (April 1999): 71.

10. Many of the training manuals used by Cuban baseball are years out of date. For example, see *Béisbol* by Juan Ealo de la Herrán (Havana: Editorial Pueblo y Educación, 1990). After a brief history of the origins of baseball in both the United States and Cuba, and a list of the various world amateur championships won by Cuban teams, Ealo devotes almost 250 pages to the fundamentals of hitting, fielding, and pitching, as well as to strategies of the game. In addition to being dated, the training techniques are heavily influenced by Eastern European and Soviet models. Cuban coaches do encounter new ideas through their contact with baseball programs in Japan, Mexico, Italy, and their occasional games with amateur teams from the United States. They would like to have some of their coaches go to spring training with U.S. teams, but as long as that remains impossible, they study the latest videos and books on technique by Tom House, Randy Johnson, Nolan Ryan, and Tony Gwynn.

11. Pettavino and Pye, *Sport in Cuba*, 142.

12. *Integración de la preselección nacional de béisbol* (Havana: Comisión Nacional de Béisbol, 1994), 1.

4. *How Ten Million Managers Learn about Baseball*

1. Quirk, *Fidel Castro*, 201.

2. Sigfredo Barros told me that the *esquina caliente* refers to any place where people congregate and talk baseball. It can be in the university, the office, or in a park. González Echevarría explains that there were references to people gathering to talk about baseball in Havana's cafes over one hundred years ago (González Echevarría, *Pride of Havana*, 109).

3. In 1995, I gave Marcelo's name to National Public Radio (NPR) producer Peter Breslow, who was going to Cuba on another assignment. Marcelo was featured in an NPR program on Cuban baseball that aired February 18, 1995.

4. "The Power Back Home," *New York Times*, 5 August 1992. On July 4, 1992, I woke up in Havana to see programming from Miami on Cuban television. Although the images were grainy, I could see *Good Morning America* and the *Today Show*. They didn't stay on long because the electricity was cut. Several Cubans told me that they believed Fidel cut it off so that they would not be able to see U.S. television. The reason for the cutoff was, however, the more serious problem of electricity shortages.

On the same day in Miami, Cuban television programs were seen on some Miami channels. Evidently, atmospheric conditions occasionally allow television signals to reach much further than the normal 150-mile range. Many people in Miami thought there might be a more sinister motive: Fidel adding more power to his transmitters. This atmospheric phenomena might account for reports by several fans in Havana that they occasionally pick up Marlins games on their regular television sets.

5. Radio Martí is a U.S. government radio station that broadcasts to Cuba in Spanish. It was created by an act of Congress in 1983 and transmitted its first broadcast on May 20, 1985. While the Radio Martí signal is jammed by the Cuban government, it is, nonetheless, heard by many people throughout the island. It carried only one game of the 1997 World Series. TV Martí began transmission in 1990, but the transmissions have never been received in Cuba because the signal is easy to block out. Thus, when NBC announcers claimed during the 1997 World Series that the TV Martí signal was blocked by the Cuban government, they were correct, but it was nothing new—simply a continuation of an old policy.

6. Occasionally Radio Rebelde can even be heard in central Texas. In 1993, I was driving from San Antonio to Austin at about 9:15 P.M. I was staying awake by alternately listening to the Astros-Dodgers game and the San Antonio Missions-Midland game. The Missions game on 680 was beginning to fade and I moved the dial to 670-Radio Rebelde. For a few seconds the signal was crystal clear, and I could hear Roberto Pacheco and Ramón Rivera broadcasting a game between the Cuban national team and Team USA live and direct from Estadio José Antonio Huelga in Sancti Spíritus. All I heard was Omar Ajete pitching the very last strike, and the game was over. Roberto then turned it over to Ramón, who did the wrap-up. Ajete was the winner, Osvaldo Fer-

nández started, and the Cubans had won the first two games of the three-game series in Cuba. The announcers then sent it back to *Deportivamente*, and the signal faded. It was indeed something from the twilight zone.

7. While few Cubans are familiar with the Internet, almost everyone sees films. There have been three Cuban productions on baseball in the past twenty years. The best is *En tres y dos* (1985), a feature-length dramatic account of a Cuban baseball player who decides to retire when his skill level begins to drop. *Redonda y viene en caja cuadrada* (1979) is a ten-minute documentary featuring game action and fan reaction, while *El que siempre pierde* (1988) is a nine-minute documentary dealing with the difficult job of an umpire in Cuban baseball.

5. "We Woke Up from the Dream Too Late": Crisis in Cuban Baseball

1. "There were perhaps 5,000 fans in the Estadio at the start of the Las Villas-Havana doubleheader," wrote Ron Fimrite in *Sports Illustrated* in 1977, "but by the beginning of the second game, their number had increased to about 20,000, close to the average crowd for games in the ball park." Ron Fimrite, "In Cuba, It's Viva El Grand Old Game," *Sports Illustrated*, 6 June 1977, 79.

2. Marelys Valencia Almeida, "Admission Charges at All Sports Events," *Granma International* (English ed.), 11 January 1995, 11. The article claimed that Cuba was the only country that did not charge admission to sporting events, but that "current economic conditions" required that the measure be taken to help stabilize the economy.

3. Pettavino and Pye, *Sport in Cuba*, 89–90.

4. See Rick Lawes, "Cuba's Toughest Opponent Is Complacency," *USA Today Baseball Weekly*, 4 August 1993, 42; Rick Lawes, "Cuban Armor Shows Its Age," *USA Today Baseball Weekly*, 17 July 1996, 31; and Larry Rohter, "No Joy in Cuba, as Its Baseball Team Strikes Out," *New York Times*, 3 November 1997.

5. Pablo Alfonso, "Apatía general se extiende a los peloteros," *El Nuevo Herald*, 13 April 1997.

6. Enrique Capetillo, "Galimatías beisbolero," *Bohemia*, 4 July 1997, B32–33.

7. One concern that was never brought up in the press, radio, or in my conversations with fans was the possibility that players might be tempted to take money to influence the outcome of games. There were scandals involving players being paid to alter the outcomes of games in Cuba in 1978 and 1982. In 1978, twenty-five players, including Bárbaro Garbey, who came to the United States during the Mariel Boat Lift and went on to play for the Detroit Tigers, were banned for life from Cuban baseball. Garbey was the first

Cuban to reach the big leagues since Tony Oliva in 1964. For details, see Herm Weiskopf, "Now it's Yanqui sí, Cuba no," *Sports Illustrated*, 13 June 1983, 58–59; and Joe Lapointe, "A Cuban with Clout," *New York Times*, 7 May 1984. In 1982, seventeen players and coaches received lifetime bans. *Latin America Weekly Report*, 2 April 1982, 4.

8. William C. Rhoden, "You Need an Olympic Coach? Cuba May Have the Answer," *New York Times*, 8 August 1992; Miguel Hernández, "Changes in Cuban Sports Not a New Policy," *Granma International* (English ed.), 17 January 1993; and Miguel Hernández, "We Must Expand Our Options, *Granma International* (English ed.), 29 January 1997.

9. Sigfredo Barros, "Trece peloteros cubanos jugarán en Japón e Italia," *Granma*, 5 May 1995.

10. Juan O. Tamayo, "Cuba Sending 50 Top Baseball Players to Japan," *Miami Herald*, 1 November 1997.

11. Carlos Cayetano, "Por qué se hundió el Titanic?" *Trabajadores*, 8 September 1997; and "El Titanic puede salir a flote," *Trabajadores*, 15 September 1997.

12. See Julie Marie Bunck, *Fidel Castro and the Quest for a Revolutionary Culture in Cuba* (University Park: Pennsylvania State University Press, 1994), 4. Bunck discusses the Cuban concept of "new man," which is based upon Vladimir Lenin's model of the ideal citizen. This person would be selfless, obedient, hardworking, incorruptible, nonmaterialistic, and loyal to the government. *Cuadros* are those who give leadership to the "new man."

13. Ernesto Guevara, "El cuadro, columna vertebral de la Revolución," in *Ernesto Che Guevara: Obras 1957–1967* (Havana: Casa de las Américas, 1970), 154–60.

6. The Defectors

1. Milton Jamail, "Bonus Babies Take First Steps," *USA Today Baseball Weekly*, 31 July 1996, 19; and Milton Jamail, "Tough Love: Rodríguez Knew Leaving Family Was the Best Way to Help Them," *USA Today Baseball Weekly*, 29 January 1997, 22.

2. Sugden, *Boxing and Society*, 144–45.

3. The only other player to appear in games at age fifteen was pitcher Jorge Luis Rivero, who was on the Industriales with Arocha.

4. Arocha returned to the game with Mérida and Monterrey in the Mexican League in 1999.

5. Charlie Nobles, "Five Cuban Players in Search of a Team," *New York Times*, 2 June 1993.

6. In a letter dated November 11, 1992, to the Commissioner of Baseball, attorney Gary Fidler outlined why the three Cubans met the definition of unrestricted free agents. A copy of the letter was sent to all twenty-eight

major league organizations and the Major League Baseball Players Association. Mr. Fidler provided a copy of the letter to the author.

When four Cuban players defected while their team played in Curaçao in 1993, a new dimension was added to the equation. "If they were to gain resident status or citizenship in the Caribbean island, they would presumably have the status of any other foreign player not subject to the draft, and would be free to sign with anyone," wrote Murray Chass in the *New York Times* (19 November 1993). This was two years before Joe Cubas took the step of gaining residency for Cuban players in a third country to make those players he represented free agents.

7. The Mets media guide states that Ordóñez played for the Cuban National Team. This was really Cuba B. Mesa was on *equipo Cuba* at Millington. For details on Ordóñez's family in Cuba, see James C. McKinley, Jr., "Cuban Players Defect, but Often With a Cost," *New York Times*, 25 April 1999.

8. *Béisbol: Guía oficial Cuba 1998* (Havana: Editorial Deportes, INDER, 1998), 240.

9. Rick Lawes and Milton Jamail, "Defecting Cuban's True Age in Dispute," *USA Today Baseball Weekly*, 17 July 1996, 31; see also Murray Chass, "Counting Cubans' Hits, Runs and Birthdays," *New York Times*, 27 April 1997.

10. Kevin Baxter, "Throwing Cuban Players a Lifeline," *Sporting News*, 10 August 1998, 21.

11. Kevin Baxter, "Making a Pitch to Hollywood," *Los Angeles Times*, 18 October 1998.

12. "New Breed of Unscrupulous Traders," *Granma International* (English ed.), 13 November 1996.

7. The Defection of the Banned

1. All three of these adjectives were actually in one article, but similar descriptions abound. Flip Bondy, "Just One Start, But Hernández Socks it to 'em," *New York Daily News*, 4 June 1998.

2. William Branigan, "No U.S. Asylum for 5 Cubans Left in Bahamian Jail," *Washington Post*, 3 January 1998.

3. L. Jon Wertheim and Don Yaeger, "Fantastic Voyage," *Sports Illustrated*, 30 November 1998, 60–63. See also Kenneth Shouler, "El Duque's Excellent Adventures," *Cigar Aficionado*, April 1999, 78–96.

4. Juan O. Tamayo, "Cubans Forsaking Rafts, Hiring Smugglers," *Miami Herald*, 28 March 1998.

5. "Información del INDER al Pueblo," *Granma*, 22 July 1997.

6. Chinea was among those banned along with Toca. This group also included Eduardo Paret, Cuba's shortstop on the gold medal team in Atlanta in 1996. Paret did not defect, and his suspension from baseball was lifted in March 1998.

7. Without mentioning Cubas by name, the *Miami Herald* reported that U.S. sports agents may have financed the defection of the Toca group. Tamayo, "Cubans Forsaking Rafts, Hiring Smugglers."

8. Bonnie DeSimone, "Bolting for a New Home: Baseball's Tug, Cuba's Ban Pull Apart Families." *Chicago Tribune*, 3 May 1998.

9. DeSimone, "Bolting for a New Home."

10. "Cuba Cancels Baseball Tour to Nicaragua," *Miami Herald*, 4 June 1998.

11. S. I. Price, "What Price Freedom?", *Sports Illustrated*, 30 March 1998, 43.

8. The Return of Rendimiento: The 37th and 38th Series Nacionales

1. Cayetano, "El Titanic puede salir a flote."

2. Martin Hacthoun, "El terreno tendrá la última palabra," *Trabajadores*, 2 March 1998.

3. Hacthoun, "El terreno tendrá la última palabra."

4. Originally known as Stadium del Cerro, or El Gran Stadium del Cerro, or Gran Stadium de La Habana, it had a capacity of thirty thousand. In addition to baseball, Cubans have packed the stadium to see various events, from a exhibition match featuring boxer Joe Louis to a concert by pianist Liberace. In 1960, the name was changed to Estadio Latinoamericano, and in 1971, it was expanded to its present capacity of fifty-five thousand to sixty thousand, depending on how many fans are squeezed into the outfield bleachers.

5. Larry Rohter, "No Joy in Cuba, as Its Baseball Team Strikes Out," *New York Times*, 3 November 1997.

9. "Bring on the Gold Rush": Major League Baseball and Cuba

1. "Nats Execute Triple Play, Win by 8–3," *Washington Post*, 24 July 1960; and Tom Miller, "Little Havana's Triple Play," *Hemispheres*, April 1993, 68–71. For details on Joe Cambria, see González Echevarría, *Pride of Havana*, 268–70.

2. Tracy Ringolsby, "Cubans Didn't Cross Water on Foot," *Baseball America*, 8 January 1996, 11; see also Tracy Ringolsby, "Mystique Makes Teams Ignore Questions of Talent," *Baseball America*, 31 May 1999, 15.

3. Frank Finch, "Drysdale Hurls as L.A. Beats Reds in Havana," *Los Angeles Times*, 21 March 1959.

4. Marcelo Sánchez sent me several clips from unidentified Havana newspapers, which were undated, describing the proposed Baltimore-Cincinnati series. See González Echevarría, *Pride of Havana*, 345, for more on the canceled Baltimore-Cincinnati series. Marcelo also sent a January 7, 1957 clip from an unidentified Havana newspaper that described the efforts of Cincinnati Reds owner Powell Crosley, Jr., and the club's general manager, Gabe Paul,

to open a training camp on the Isle of Pines (now Isla de la Juventud). The plan was to have the Cincinnati team train there and play exhibition games against Cuban teams before they returned to Florida for spring training exhibition games.

5. Edward Boorstein, *The Economic Transformation of Cuba* (New York: Monthly Review Press, 1968), 28–29.

6. "Ball Stars' Tour of Cuba Is Sought," *New York Times*, 2 May 1971.

7. Memo William Rogers to Henry Kissinger, 13 February 1975. This is one of eighteen secret documents that were made public by the National Security Archive in early 1999 and are posted on their website (www.seas. gwu.edu/nsarchive/).

8. Memo from William Rogers to Henry Kissinger, 13 February 1975.

9. Department of State, Secret/NODIS Memorandum, 19 February 1975. Cited in Peter Kornbluh, "Here's the Windup: Scouting a Lefty Named Castro," *Washington Post*, 17 January 1999.

10. Memo, "Outline of Cuban Exhibition Game Proposal," 13 June 1975. This is also one of the secret documents that were made public by the National Security Archive.

11. Les Brown, "U.S. Cancels Cuban Baseball Telecast," *New York Times*, 7 January 1976.

12. "State Department Not Opposed to Yanks Visiting Cuba," *New York Times*, 5 March 1977.

13. Personal interview with Wayne Smith, 28 October 1988.

14. Murray Chass, "Behind the Kuhn-Cuba Tangle," *New York Times*, 12 March 1977.

15. Chass, "Behind the Kuhn-Cuba Tangle."

16. "Indians Seeking to Play Cubans," *New York Times*, 2 March 1978; and "Indians vs. Cuba Series Snagged," *New York Times*, 24 March 1978.

17. "Mariners Absolve Kuhn," *New York Times*, 22 January 1982.

18. After meetings with LULAC (League of United Latin American Citizens) in Havana in 1984, the Cuban government announced that it was willing to play an exhibition series against any major league team. Mario Obledo, "It's Time for Baseball Diplomacy," *Latino* (LULAC) 56, no. 1 (Winter 1984–85): 6.

19. In 1999, two Cuban players, Juan Díaz and Josué Pérez who had been signed by the Los Angeles Dodgers in 1995, were declared free agents by Major League Baseball, which ruled that the two players were signed in violation of the Kuhn Directive.

20. Houston Astros president Tal Smith has had an ongoing interest in Cuba since the late 1950s. He began his baseball career with the Cincinnati Reds in 1958. At the time, the Reds had a working agreement with Marianao in the Cuban League and the Cuban Sugar Kings of the Triple A International League.

21. Murray Chass, "Yanks Upset as Kuhn Vetoes Their Cuba Trip," *New York Times*, 9 March 1977.

22. Smith, *The Closest of Enemies*, 191.

23. U.S. Department of the Treasury, Office of Foreign Assets Control, *What You Need to Know about the U.S. Embargo: An Overview of the Cuban Assets Control Regulations. Title 31 Part 514 of the U.S. Code of Federal Regulations* (Washington, D.C.: U.S. Government Printing Office, 1996).

The May/June 1999 issue of *Cigar Aficionado* is devoted almost entirely to Cuba. Included in the coverage are articles by U.S. Senators Christopher Dodd (D-CT) and Jesse Helms (R-NC), as well as an article by Ricardo Alarcón, president of Cuba's National Assembly, examining the effects of the embargo.

10. Beyond the Embargo and Fidel

1. Rich Oppel, "Castro Asks for Cut of Baseball Action," *Austin American-Statesman*, 25 October 1998.

2. Associated Press, 2 November 1998.

3. Jorge Morejón, "'El Gallego' infla globo de grandes ligas," *El Nuevo Herald*, 2 January 1999.

4. H.R. 9, 105th Congress, 1st sess.

5. David Beard, "Legislation Would Let Cubans Play in the U.S. Without Defecting," *Fort Lauderdale Sun-Sentinel*, 28 January 1997.

6. Currently, each major league team is allowed approximately thirty labor certifications from the U.S. Department of Labor to bring in minor league players. Major league players come under a different category and are not limited by a quota. It is not clear how a large influx of Cuban players would affect the current system. See Milton Jamail, "Government Quota Creates Visa Bottleneck for Players," *Baseball America*, 2 March 1998, 12.

7. There is at least one other country from which athletes must defect in order to compete in U.S. professional sports: North Korea. Michael Ri, whose real name is Ri Myong Hun, is a 7'9" North Korean citizen with dreams of playing in the National Basketball Association. His dreams are on hold because the Clinton administration will not allow him to come to the United States to play unless he defects, something he is unwilling to do. Barbara Smith, "Hoops Player Waits on Diplomatic Jump Ball," *USA Today*, 1 April 1998.

8. Miguel Hernández, "Lo primero es nuestra concepción del hombre," *Granma*, 22 April 1998.

9. Aesop, *Belling the Cat and Other Aesop's Fables*, retold in verse by Tom Paxton (New York: Morrow Junior Books, 1990).

10. Because the summer Olympic games are held during baseball season, the best professional players competing in the United States are not available to play. It is likely that a World Cup featuring teams from the United States, Japan, Puerto Rico, the Dominican Republic, Venezuela, and Cuba, among

others, will be organized after the World Series. No specific timetable has been set for the first tournament.

11. González Echevarría, *Pride of Havana*, 337–39, describes the atmosphere in Havana in the late 1940s when Cuban baseball officials were positioning themselves to seek a major league franchise.

Epilogue: From the Bay of Pigs to Baltimore

1. In February 1999, the U.S. State Department, citing ongoing negotiations concerning the Orioles game, denied permission for 1998 American League MVP Juan González to travel to Cuba to conduct baseball clinics.

2. Jim Hoagland, "Tiptoeing 'Round a Relic," *Washington Post*, 7 January 1999. See also Frank Davies, "White House Considers Plan for a Commission to Carry Out a Bipartisan Review," *Miami Herald*, 24 November 1998; Juan O. Tamayo, "U.S. Sanctions on Cuba Under Growing Attack," *Miami Herald*, 20 December 1998; and William Ratliff, "A New 'Kissinger Commission' on Cuba," *Wall Street Journal*, 23 October 1998.

3. Personal correspondence with Marcelo Sánchez, 21 January 1999.

4. *Granma*, 4 May 1999.

5. González Echevarría, *Pride of Havana*, 206–7.

6. *Granma*, 6 May 1999, printed the entire text of the speech.

7. González Echevarría, *Pride of Havana*, 353; and "Castro supervisa práctica de selección," *El Nuevo Herald*, 29 April 1999.

BIBLIOGRAPHY

Aesop. *Belling the Cat and Other Aesop's Fables*. Retold in verse by Tom Paxton. New York: Morrow Junior Books, 1990.

Alfonso, Jorge, and Enrique Capetillo. "Su pueblo ganó un gran conductor." *Bohemia*, 16 October 1987, 83.

Arbena, Joseph L. *Sport and Society in Latin America*. New York: Greenwood Press, 1988.

Baxter, Kevin. "Throwing Cuban Players a Lifeline." *Sporting News*, 10 August 1998, 21.

Béisbol: Guía oficial Cuba 1998. Havana: Editorial Deportes, INDER, 1998.

Bjarkman, Peter. *Baseball and Castro's Revolution*. Jefferson, N.C.: McFarland, forthcoming.

———. "Baseball and Fidel Castro." *National Pastime: A Review of Baseball History* 18 (1998): 64–68.

———. *Baseball with a Latin Beat*. Jefferson, N.C: McFarland, 1994.

Bjarkman, Peter, and Mark Rucker. *Smoke: The Romance and Lore of Cuban Baseball*. New York: Total Sports, 1999.

Boorstein, Edward. *The Economic Transformation of Cuba*. New York: Monthly Review Press, 1968.

Boswell, Thomas. *How Life Imitates the World Series*. New York: Penguin, 1983.

Brock, Lisa, and Bijan Bayne. "Not Just Black: African Americans, Cubans and Baseball." In *Between Race and Empire: African-Americans and Cubans Before the Cuban Revolution*, edited by Lisa Brock and Digna Castañeda Fuertes, 186–204, Philadelphia: Temple University Press, 1998.

Brown, Bruce. "Cuban Baseball." *Atlantic*, 6 June 1984, 109–14.

Bunck, Julie Marie. *Fidel Castro and the Quest for a Revolutionary Culture in Cuba*. University Park: Pennsylvania State University Press, 1994.

Burgos, Adrian, Jr. "Jugando en el norte: Caribbean Players in the Negro Leagues, 1910–1950." *Centro: Journal of the Center for Puerto Rican Studies* 8, nos. 1 & 2 (1996): 128–49.

Capetillo, Enrique. "Galimatías beisbolero." *Bohemia*, 4 July 1997, B32–33.

Casas, Edel, Jorge Alfonso, and Alberto Pestana. *Viva y en juego*. Havana: Ministro de Cultura, Editorial Científico-Técnica, 1986.

Clark, Dick, and Larry Lester, eds. *The Negro Leagues Book*. Cleveland: Society for American Baseball Research, 1994.

Delgado, Gabino, and Severo Nieto. *Béisbol cubano: Récords y estadísticas*. Havana: Editorial Lex, 1955.

Ealo de la Herrán, Juan. *Béisbol*. Havana: Editorial Pueblo y Educación, 1990.

Fimrite, Ron. "In Cuba, It's Viva El Grand Old Game." *Sports Illustrated*, 6 June 1977, 79.

González Echevarría, Roberto. "The '47 Dodgers in Havana: Baseball at a Crossroads." *1996 Spring Training Baseball Yearbook* 9 (Spring 1996): 20–25.

———. "The Game in Matanzas: On the Origins of Cuban Baseball." *Yale Review* 83, no. 3 (1995): 62–94.

———. *The Pride of Havana: A History of Cuban Baseball*. New York: Oxford University Press, 1999.

Guevara, Ernesto. "El cuadro, columna vertebral de la Revolución," in *Ernesto Che Guevara: Obras 1957–1967*, 154–60. Havana: Casa de las Américas, 1970.

Hernández, Luis. "Un siglo de béisbol en Cuba." *Semanario Deportivo LPV*, 2 December 1969, 8.

Hoak, Don, with Myron Cope. "The Day I Batted Against Castro." *Sport*, June 1964, 30+.

Holway, John. *Blackball Stars: Negro League Pioneers*. Westport, Conn.: Meckler Books, 1988.

Integración de la preselección nacional de béisbol. Havana: Comisión Nacional de Béisbol, 1994.

Jamail, Milton. "Bonus Babies Take First Steps." *USA Today Baseball Weekly*, 31 July 1996, 19.

———. "Government Quota Creates Visa Bottleneck for Players." *Baseball America*, 2 March 1998, 12.

———. "Tough Love: Rodriguez Knew Leaving Family Was the Best Way to Help Them." *USA Today Baseball Weekly*, 29 January 1997, 22.

Johnson, Lloyd, and Miles Wolff, eds. *The Encyclopedia of Minor League Baseball*. Durham, N.C.: Baseball America, 1993.

Joseph, Gilbert M. "Documenting a Regional Pastime: Baseball in Yucatán."

In *Windows on Latin America: Understanding Society Through Photographs*, edited by Robert M. Levine, 76–89. Coral Gables, Fla.: North-South Center, University of Miami, 1987.

Kerrane, Kevin. *Dollar Sign on the Muscle*. New York: Simon & Schuster, 1984.

Klein, Alan. *Sugarball: The American Game, the Dominican Dream*. New Haven: Yale University Press, 1991.

Lawes, Rick. "Arocha Succeeds in Breaking Down Barrier." *USA Today Baseball Weekly*, 28 July 1993, 5.

———. "Cuban Armor Shows Its Age." *USA Today Baseball Weekly*, 17 July 1996, 31.

———. "Cuba's Toughest Opponent Is Complacency." *USA Today Baseball Weekly*, 4–10 August 1993, 42.

Lawes, Rick, and Milton Jamail. "Defecting Cuban's True Age in Dispute." *USA Today Baseball Weekly*, 17 July 1996, 31.

Losada, Jess. "Hace cuarenta y seis años se jugaba baseball en Caracas." *Carteles* (Havana), 30 November 1941, 8–9.

McCarthy, Eugene. "Diamond Diplomacy." *New Republic*, 28 April 1982, 12.

Miller, Tom. "Cuba's All-Stars." *Natural History* 108, no. 33 (April 1999): 62–73.

———. "Little Havana's Triple Play." *Hemispheres*, April 1993, 68–71.

———. *Trading with the Enemy: A Yankee Travels Through Castro's Cuba*. New York: Atheneum, 1992.

Miná, Gianni. *Un encuentro con Fidel*. Havana: Oficina de Publicaciones del Consejo de Estado, 1987.

Obledo, Mario. "It's Time for Baseball Diplomacy." *Latino* (LULAC) 56, no. 1 (Winter 1984–85): 6.

Oleksak, Michael M., and Mary Adams Oleksak. *Béisbol: Latin Americans and the Grand Old Game*. Grand Rapids, Mich.: Masters Press, 1991.

Padura, Leonardo, and Raúl Arce. *El alma en el terreno: Estrellas del béisbol*. Havana: Editorial Abril, 1989.

Pettavino, Paula J., and Geralyn Pye. *Sport in Cuba: The Diamond in the Rough*. Pittsburgh: University of Pittsburgh Press, 1994.

Pérez, Louis A., Jr. "Between Baseball and Bullfighting: The Quest for Nationality in Cuba, 1868–1898," *Journal of American History* 81, no. 2 (1994): 493–517.

———. *Between Revolution and Reform*. 2d ed. New York: Oxford University Press, 1995.

Pérez-Stable, Marifeli. *The Cuban Revolution: Origins, Course, and Legacy*. New York: Oxford University Press, 1993.

Pickering, R.J. "Cuba." In *Sport under Communism*, edited by James Riordan, 141–74. Montreal: McGill-Queen's University Press, 1978.

Price, S. I. "What Price Freedom?" *Sports Illustrated*, 30 March 1998, 42–43.

Quirk, Robert. *Fidel Castro*. New York: W. W. Norton, 1993.

Ramírez Aznar, Luis. *La historia del béisbol en Yucatán*. Vol. 1. Mérida, Mexico: Novedades, 1989.

Ringolsby, Tracy. "Cubans Didn't Cross Water on Foot." *Baseball America*, 8 January 1996, 11.

————. "Mystique Makes Teams Ignore Questions of Talent." *Baseball America*, 31 May 1999, 15.

Rodríguez, Rubén. "Oye . . . a la pelota." *Semanario Deportivo LPV*, 2 March 1965, 5.

————. "Serie Nacional y IX Festival." *Semanario Deportivo LPV*, 27 April 1965, 5.

Rogosin, Don. *Invisible Men*. New York: Atheneum, 1987.

Ruck, Rob. "Baseball in the Caribbean." In *Total Baseball*, 5th ed., edited by John Thorn et al., 473–79. New York: Viking Perennial, 1997.

————. *The Tropic of Baseball: Baseball in the Dominican Republic*. Westport, Conn.: Meckler, 1991.

Santana Alonso, Alfredo. *El inmortal del béisbol: Martín Dihigo*. Havana: Editorial Científico-Técnica, 1998.

Shouler, Kenneth. "El Duque's Excellent Adventures." *Cigar Aficionado*, April 1999, 78–96.

Smith, Wayne. *The Closest of Enemies*. New York: W. W. Norton, 1987.

Sugden, John. *Boxing and Society: An International Analysis*. Manchester: Manchester University Press, 1996.

Szulc, Tad. *Fidel: A Critical Portrait*. New York: William Morrow, 1987.

Torres, Angel. *La leyenda del béisbol cubano*. Los Angeles: the author, 1997.

Truby, David J. "Castro's Curveball." *Harper's*, May 1989, 32–33.

U.S. Department of the Treasury. Office of Foreign Assets Control. *What You Need to Know about the U.S. Embargo: An Overview of the Cuban Assets Control Regulations. Title 31 Part 514 of the U.S. Code of Federal Regulations*. Washington, D.C.: U.S. Government Printing Office, 1996.

U.S. House Subcommittee on Inter-American Affairs of the Committee on Foreign Relations. *Soviet Naval Activities in Cuba*. 91st Cong., 2nd sess., 26 September 1971.

U.S. Senate Select Committee to Study Governmental Operations with Respect to Intelligence Activities. *Alleged Assassination Plots Involving Foreign Leaders*. Washington, D.C.: U.S. Government Printing Office, 1975.

Valdez, Tirso A. *Notas acerca del béisbol dominicano del pasado y del presente*. Ciudad Trujillo, Dominican Republic: Editorial del Caribe, 1958.

Wagner, Eric A. "Baseball in Cuba." *Journal of Popular Culture* 18, no. 1 (1984): 113–20.

————. "Sport in Revolutionary Societies: Cuba and Nicaragua." In *Sport and Society in Latin America*, edited by Joseph L. Arbena, 113–36. New York: Greenwood Press, 1988.

Weiskopf, Herm. "Now It's Yanqui sí, Cuba no." *Sports Illustrated*, 13 June 1983, 58+.

Wertheim, L. Jon, and Don Yaeger. "Fantastic Voyage." *Sports Illustrated*, 30 November 1998, 60–63.

INDEX

Milton H. Jamail is a lecturer in the Department of Government at the University of Texas at Austin. Since the early 1990s, he has been a regular contributor to *USA Today Baseball Weekly* and *Baseball America*. His articles on Latin American baseball have also appeared in *Hispanic*, the *Houston Chronicle*, *Texas Monthly*, and the *Washington Post*.